혼공 기초구문

혼공 기초구문

허준석·신영환 지음

L2

혼공북스

혼공 기초 구문 Level 2

1판 1쇄 2022년 2월 7일
1판 2쇄 2023년 1월 2일

지은이   허준석 신영환
디자인   박새롬
표지그림   김효지
마케팅   김보미 정경훈
브랜드   혼공북스
펴낸곳   (주)혼공유니버스
출판등록   제2021-000288호
주   소   04033 서울특별시 마포구 양화로 113 4층(서교동)
전자메일   admin@hongong.co.kr

ISBN   979-11-976810-1-1   13740

혼공!

눈앞에 맛있는 소고기가 있어요. 너무 배고파서 바로 먹고 싶은데 고기가 너무 커서 한 입에 넣을 수가 없어요. 이럴 때 어떻게 해야 하죠?

맞아요. 작게 잘라서 한 입에 쏘옥 넣어서 먹으면 되지요.

영어 읽기도 마찬가지예요. 긴 영어 글을 한방에 읽고 핵심만 쏙쏙 이해하고 싶잖아요? 하지만 긴 글을 한 호흡에 읽어나가는 것은 쉽지가 않아요. 그렇기 때문에 쌤이 말한 소고기의 원리를 적용해 봅시다. 글을 한 입에 들어갈 수 있을 정도의 작은 단위로 잘라보는 거예요. 그 적당한 크기를 보통 문장이라고 하지요.

이렇게 영어 글을 문장 단위로 잘라서 공부하는 것을 구문공부 또는 구문독해라고 해요. 원서 읽기를 술술술 해내는 친구들에게는 필요가 없을 수도 있지만, 한국에서 자란 많은 친구들에게는 한 번쯤 꼬옥 해볼 것을 권한답니다.

특히 문장을 공부하면서 그 속에서 나오는 단어, 문법을 익히고, 우리말을 보면서 영작까지 해본다면 독해는 물론, 수행평가, 지필고사의 기본기까지 한 번에 쌓을 수 있어요.

우리 친구들! 영어는 절대 어렵지 않아요. 선생님과 함께 딱 20일 동안 교재, 강의를 충실히 보고 나면 자신감이 생길 거예요. 걱정말고 즐겁게, 효율적으로 혼공 해봅시다.

이제 준비되었나요? 그럼 다 같이 Let's get it!

대표저자 | 혼공 허준석

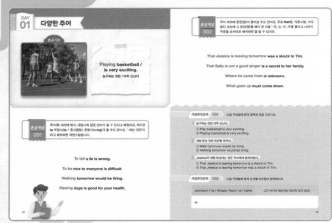

총 ④단계의 완공, 혼공 시스템!

〈혼공기초구문 레벨 2〉 미리보기

1 혼공기초

최소의 개념으로 핵심 문장을 공부해요. 적절한 분량의 예문으로 개념을 익히고, 간단한 간접 영작을 통해 적용을 해본답니다. 할 수 있다는 자신감이 생길 거예요.

2 혼공연습

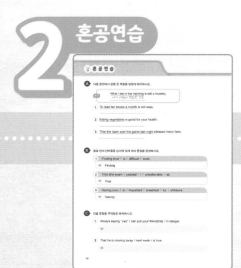

간단한 문항을 풀면서 개념을 반복 적용하고 서서히 확장시켜 나갑니다. 우리말 해석부터 힌트가 주어진 쉬운 영작까지 어렵지 않게 할 수 있어요.

3 혼공완성

실제 생활과 관련된 사진을 보면서 영작을 한 다음, 힌트가 최소화 된 영작을 하면서 가장 난도가 높은 문제까지 순서대로 다뤄요. 마지막으로, 개념이 적용된 다양한 유형의 문항을 다루면서 실전 감각을 끌어올려요.

4 혼공복습

하나의 Day 학습을 효과적으로 마무리 할 수 있는 복습 코너예요. 가장 쉬운 A문항부터, 우리말 의미에 맞게 문장이나 어구를 쓰는 좀 더 어려운 B문항까지 순서대로 제공해요. 이후 더 어려운 C문항의 영작, 마지막 우리말 의미 파악 D문항 까지 체계적으로 풀고 나면 완전학습을 할 수 있어요.

목차

하루 30~40분, 20일만에 기초구문 **완전정복**하기!

하루 30~40분 집중 학습으로 20일 동안 중학영어 과정에서 알아야 할 기초 구문을
마스터할 수 있는 Study Plan입니다. 학습 후 ◯에 V 표시 하세요.

◯ Day 01	◯ Day 02	◯ Day 03	◯ Day 04	◯ Day 05
다양한 주어	다양한 목적어	가주어 / 가목적어	다양한 보어	to 부정사의 명사적 용법 / 동명사

◯ Day 06	◯ Day 07	◯ Day 08	◯ Day 09	◯ Day 10
to 부정사의 형용사적 용법	to 부정사의 부사적 용법	to 부정사의 be to 용법	분사	분사구문

◯ Day 11	◯ Day 12	◯ Day 13	◯ Day 14	◯ Day 15
관계대명사 - 주격	관계대명사 - 목적격	관계대명사 - 소유격	관계부사 - when, where, why, how	관계사의 계속적 용법

◯ Day 16	◯ Day 17	◯ Day 18	◯ Day 19	◯ Day 20
관계대명사 what	복합관계사	비교급	원급비교	최상급 / 관용적 표현

★ 무료 유튜브 강의와 함께 학습하면 훨씬 더 효율적입니다. 아래의 **QR코드**를 찍어 보세요!

★ 더 많은 강의는 **혼공마켓 클래스룸** (https://hongong.co.kr/classroom)에서 보실 수 있습니다.

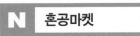

Part 1

주어/목적어/보어의 확장
다양한 주어/목적어/보어

다양한 주어

혼공기초

Playing basketball /
is very exciting.
농구하는 것은 / 아주 신난다

혼공개념
001

주어(S) 자리에 명사, 대명사와 같은 단어가 올 수 있다고 배웠어요. 하지만 **to** 부정사(**to** + 동사원형), 동명사(**v-ing**)가 올 수도 있어요. '~하는 것은'이라고 해석하면 자연스럽답니다.

To tell **a lie is wrong.**

To be **nice to everyone is difficult.**

Walking **tomorrow would be tiring.**

Raising **dogs is good for your health.**

That Jessica is leaving tomorrow was a shock to Tim.

That Sally is not a good singer is a secret to her family.

Where he came from is unknown.

What goes up must come down.

개념확인문제 001   다음 우리말에 맞게 영작한 것을 고르시오.

1 농구하는 것은 아주 신난다.

① Play basketball is very exciting.
② Playing basketball is very exciting.

2 내일 걷는 것은 피곤할 것이다.

① Walk tomorrow would be tiring.
② Walking tomorrow would be tiring.

3 Jessica가 내일 떠난다는 것은 Tim에게 충격이었다.

① That Jessica is leaving tomorrow is a shock to Tim.
② That Jessica is leaving tomorrow was a shock to Tim.

개념확인문제 002   다음 우리말에 맞게 순서를 바로잡아 영작하시오.

unknown / he / Where / from / is / came	그가 어디서 왔는지는 알려져 있지 않다.

13

A 다음 문장에서 밑줄 친 부분을 알맞게 해석하시오.

> 보기
>
> What I ate in the morning is still a mystery.
> 내가 아침에 먹었던 것은

(1) To read ten books a month is not easy.

_____

(2) Eating vegetables is good for your health.

_____

(3) That the team won the game last night pleased many fans.

_____

B 괄호 안의 단어들을 순서에 맞게 써서 문장을 완성하시오.

(1) Finding (true | is | difficult | love).

➡ Finding _____ .

(2) That (the exam | passed | I | unbelievable | is).

➡ That _____ .

(3) Having (very | is | important | breakfast | for | children).

➡ Having _____ .

C 다음 문장을 우리말로 해석하시오.

(1) Always saying "yes" / can put your friendship / in danger.

➡

(2) That he is moving away / next week / is true.

➡

🎯 혼공완성

A 사진을 보고 주어진 단어들의 순서를 바로잡아 문장을 완성하시오.

1
by law | wear | required | a seat belt | To | is

....

2
I | a cute dog | found | What | in | the park | was

....

B 주어진 단어들의 순서를 바로잡아 문장을 완성하시오.

1 was | someone's | to me | SNS | Following | annoying

➡

2 increase | Advertising | can | sales | the product

➡

3 is | one | of cancer | of the major causes | To smoke

➡

C ❶~❹의 밑줄 친 부분 중 어법상 잘못된 것 두 개의 번호를 쓰고, 각각 어법에 알맞게 고치시오.

❶ One scientist on the team for this experiment <u>were</u> Tim.
❷ French fries made by my sister <u>are</u> not salty.
❸ What is not wisdom <u>is</u> dangerous.
❹ To be happy <u>mean</u> a lot to me.

잘못된 것   **바른 표현**

_____ ➡ _____

_____ ➡ _____

A 우리말 의미를 참고하여 빈칸을 알맞게 채우시오. 🔍 잘 모르겠다면 ···→ 13페이지로

① 농구하는 것은 아주 신난다.

　　　　　　　　　　 basketball is very 　　　　　　　 .

② 내일 걷는 것은 피곤할 것이다.

　　　　　　　　　　 tomorrow would be 　　　　　　　 .

③ Jessica가 내일 떠난다는 것은 Tim에게 충격이었다.

That Jessica is 　　　　　　 tomorrow was a 　　　　　　 to Tim.

④ 그가 어디서 왔는지는 알려져 있지 않다.

　　　　　　　　　　 he came from is 　　　　　　 .

B 다음 우리말에 맞게 순서를 바로잡아 영작하시오. 🔍 잘 모르겠다면 ···→ 14페이지로

① 채소를 먹는 것은 당신의 건강에 좋다.
is | for | your health | good | vegetables | eating

➡

② 진정한 사랑을 찾는 것은 어렵다.
true | is | difficult | finding | love

➡

③ 내가 시험에 합격했다는 것은 믿을 수 없다.
the exam | passed | I | that | unbelievable | is

➡

④ 아침 식사를 하는 것은 아이들에게 아주 중요하다.
very | is | important | having | breakfast | for | children

➡

C 주어진 단어들의 순서를 바로잡아 문장을 완성하시오.
잘 모르겠다면 ···· 15페이지로

1 by law | wear | required | a seat belt | to | is
➡

2 I | a cute dog | found | what | in | the park | was
➡

3 was | someone's | to me | SNS | following | annoying
➡

4 increase | advertising | can | sales | the product
➡

5 is | one | of cancer | of the major causes | to smoke
➡

D 다음 ❶~❹의 우리말 뜻을 적으시오.
잘 모르겠다면 ···· 15페이지로

❶ One scientist on the team for this experiment was Tim.
❷ French fries made by my sister are not salty.
❸ What is not wisdom is dangerous.
❹ To be happy means a lot to me.

1 _____

2 _____

3 _____

4 _____

혼공기초

She desired / to become a soccer player.
그녀는 바랐다 / 축구 선수가 되는 것을

혼공개념 001

많은 동사들 뒤에는 우리말로 '을, 를'에 해당하는 것이 올 수 있어요. 이를 목적어(**O**)라 부르고, 명사, 대명사, **to** 부정사(**to** + 동사원형), 동명사 (**v-ing**)가 올 수 있어요.

I enjoyed the amazing views of the city at night.

Daniel invited us to his first concert.

You will begin to feel happy about yourself.

He stopped talking about his strength.

목적어 자리에 문장(절)이 들어갈 수도 있어요. 주로 **that**절, 의문사절, 기타 절이 오는데 그 문장(절)을 해석 한 다음 '~을, 를'을 붙이면 해석이 잘 돼요.

Did you know that African elephants are disappearing?

You are showing that you are interested in the other person.

No one knows what will happen in the future.

We decided what we should eat first.

개념확인문제 001 다음 우리말에 맞게 영작한 것을 고르시오.

1 그녀는 축구 선수가 되는 것을 바랐다.

① She desires to become a soccer player.
② She desired to become a soccer player.

2 그는 그의 힘에 대해 말하는 것을 멈췄다.

① He stopped talking about his strength.
② He talking stopped about his strength.

3 너는 아프리카 코끼리가 사라지고 있는 중이라는 것을 알았니?

① Did you knew that African elephants are disappearing?
② Did you know that African elephants are disappearing?

개념확인문제 002 다음 우리말에 맞게 순서를 바로잡아 영작하시오.

in the future / knows / will happen / what / No one	미래에 무슨 일이 일어날지 아무도 모른다.

19

A 다음 문장에서 밑줄 친 부분을 알맞게 해석하시오.

> 보기
> She started to paint the flag.
> <u>그 깃발에 색칠하는 것을</u>

1 She prepared a turkey for Thanksgiving.

_____

2 They discussed the difficulty of studying abroad.

_____

3 I asked if she could speak French.

_____

B 괄호 안의 단어들을 순서에 맞게 써서 문장을 완성하시오.

1 She (her | painted | with a paintbrush | self-portrait).

➡ She _____ .

2 I (the picture | a great cost | bought | at).

➡ I _____ .

3 She (her hand | raised | above her head).

➡ She _____ .

C 다음 문장을 우리말로 해석하시오.

1 He wonders / if the rich are really happy.

➡

2 You will want / to set new goals and / to try new things.

➡

A 사진을 보고 주어진 단어들의 순서를 바로잡아 문장을 완성하시오.

1

cooking classes | in her community | started | teaching | She

....

2

The scientists | wrong | figured out | went | what

....

B 주어진 단어들의 순서를 바로잡아 문장을 완성하시오.

1 what | doesn't | Phillip | know | happened | to Janet

➡

2 why | tell | you | I | chose | I'll | this subject

➡

3 care | She | she | how | dresses | doesn't

➡

C ❶~❹의 밑줄 친 부분 중 어법상 잘못된 것 두 개의 번호를 쓰고, 각각 어법에 알맞게 고치시오.

❶ Henry enjoys <u>plays</u> the violin.
❷ She decided <u>to study</u> hard.
❸ Many people believe <u>that</u> clovers with four leaves are lucky.
❹ I don't know <u>that</u> he is at home or not.

잘못된 것   바른 표현

_____ _____

_____ _____

A 우리말 의미를 참고하여 빈칸을 알맞게 채우시오.

🔍 잘 모르겠다면 …→ 19페이지로

(1) 그녀는 축구 선수가 되는 것을 바랐다.

She _____ to _____ a soccer player.

(2) 그는 그의 힘에 대해 말하는 것을 멈췄다.

He _____ talking about his _____ .

(3) 너는 아프리카 코끼리가 사라지고 있는 중이라는 것을 알았니?

Did you _____ that African elephants are _____ ?

(4) 미래에 무슨 일이 일어날지 아무도 모른다.

No one _____ what will _____ in the future.

B 다음 우리말에 맞게 순서를 바로잡아 영작하시오.

🔍 잘 모르겠다면 …→ 20페이지로

(1) 그들은 해외에서 공부하는 것의 어려움에 대해 논의했다.
the difficulty | discussed | of studying abroad | they

➡

(2) 나는 그 그림을 비싼 가격에 샀다.
the picture | a great cost | bought | I | at

➡

(3) 그는 부자들이 정말 행복한지 궁금해한다.
happy | are | wonders | the rich | he | if | really

➡

(4) 너는 새로운 목표들을 정하고 새로운 것들을 시도하기를 원하게 될 것이다.
to set | want | will | and | to try | you | new things | new goals

➡

Q 잘 모르겠다면 … 21페이지로

C 주어진 단어들의 순서를 바로잡아 문장을 완성하시오.

1 cooking classes | in her community | started | teaching | she

➡

2 the scientists | wrong | figured out | went | what

➡

3 what | doesn't | Phillip | know | happened | to Janet

➡

4 why | tell | you | I | chose | I'll | this subject

➡

5 care | she | she | how | dresses | doesn't

➡

Q 잘 모르겠다면 … 21페이지로

D 다음 ❶~❹의 우리말 뜻을 적으시오.

❶ Henry enjoys playing the violin.

❷ She decided to study hard.

❸ Many people believe that clovers with four leaves are lucky.

❹ I don't know if he is at home or not.

1 _____

2 _____

3 _____

4 _____

혼공기초

It is important /
to stay healthy.
중요하다 / 건강을 유지하는 것은

혼공개념
001

주어 자리의 **it**이 중요한 의미를 가지지 않을 때 가주어라고 하고, 뒤에 따라오는 **to** + 동사원형 이하 또는 **that**절 이하를 진주어라고 해요. 진주어 다음에 '~은, 는'을 붙여 해석하면 자연스럽답니다.

It is hard to study English alone.

It is useful to talk to someone about your problems.

It is surprising that whales are mammals.

It is not helpful that we have two old cars.

목적어 자리의 **it**이 중요한 의미를 가지지 않을 때 가목적어라고 하고, 뒤에 따라오는 **to** + 동사원형 이하 또는 **that**절 이하 등을 진목적어라고 해요. **make, think, believe, consider, find** 등과 같은 동사를 쓰는 문장에서 자주 등장해요.

She found it difficult to breathe.

The rain made it difficult to drive.

He made it clear that we should leave.

I consider it important that we need to encourage people.

개념확인문제 001 다음 우리말에 맞게 영작한 것을 고르시오.

1 건강을 유지하는 것은 중요하다.

① It is important stay healthy.
② It is important to stay healthy.

2 고래가 포유류라는 것은 놀라운 일이다.

① It is surprising if whales are mammals.
② It is surprising that whales are mammals.

3 비는 운전하는 것을 어렵게 만들었다.

① The rain made it difficult to drive.
② The rain made that difficult to drive.

개념확인문제 002 다음 우리말에 맞게 순서를 바로잡아 영작하시오.

leave / He / it / clear / we / should / that / made

그는 우리가 떠나야 한다는 것을 분명히 했다.

➜

25

혼공연습

A 다음 문장에서 밑줄 친 부분을 알맞게 해석하시오.

> 보기
> It is so important <u>to believe in yourself</u>.
> <u>너 자신을 믿는 것은</u>

(1) It is possible <u>to float in water</u>.

_____

(2) It is better <u>to say "no" and explain why</u>.

_____

(3) It is difficult <u>for teenagers to fall asleep before midnight</u>.

_____

B 괄호 안의 단어들을 순서에 맞게 써서 문장을 완성하시오.

(1) I (it | a teacher | hard | thought | to become).

➡ I _____ .

(2) It (for parents | natural | to want | is | their children | to protect).

➡ It _____ .

(3) It (that | bad | true | some habits | is | are | for us).

➡ It _____ .

C 다음 문장을 우리말로 해석하시오.

(1) His attitude / made it difficult / to work together.

➡

(2) Many people / don't consider it important / to recycle.

➡

혼공완성

A 사진을 보고 주어진 단어들의 순서를 바로잡아 문장을 완성하시오.

1

Sean | is | our club | sad | that | cannot join | It

....

2

It | shoes | is | in a living room | fine | for Americans | to wear

....

B 주어진 단어들의 순서를 바로잡아 문장을 완성하시오.

1 very important | to exercise | It | regularly | is

➡

2 efficiency | makes | This machine | possible | to increase | it

➡

3 made | for them | it | difficult | The weather | to stay warm

➡

C ❶~❹의 밑줄 친 부분 중 성격이 다른 하나를 골라 번호를 쓰고, 그 문장 전체를 우리말로 해석하시오.

❶ It is a good idea to choose something interesting.
❷ Andy found it almost impossible to fix the computer.
❸ It is difficult to do your homework without any help.
❹ It was difficult for the boy to hear the whistle.

번호: _____

해석: _____

혼공복습

A 우리말 의미를 참고하여 빈칸을 알맞게 채우시오.

잘 모르겠다면 … 25페이지로

(1) 건강을 유지하는 것은 중요하다.

_____ is important to _____ healthy.

(2) 고래가 포유류라는 것은 놀라운 일이다.

It is _____ that whales are _____ .

(3) 비는 운전하는 것을 어렵게 만들었다.

The _____ made it _____ to drive.

(4) 그는 우리가 떠나야 한다는 것을 분명히 했다.

He made _____ clear that we should _____ .

B 다음 우리말에 맞게 순서를 바로잡아 영작하시오.

잘 모르겠다면 … 26페이지로

(1) 물에서 떠 있는 것은 가능하다.
to float | possible | is | in water | it

➡

(2) 나는 선생님이 되는 것을 어렵다고 생각했다.
it | a teacher | hard | thought | I | to become

➡

(3) 그의 태도는 함께 일하는 것을 어렵게 만들었다.
to work together | made | his attitude | it | difficult

➡

(4) 많은 사람들은 재활용하는 것을 중요하다고 여기지 않는다.
people | don't | it | many | important | to recycle | consider

➡

잘 모르겠다면 … 27페이지로

C 주어진 단어들의 순서를 바로잡아 문장을 완성하시오.

1 Sean | is | our club | sad | that | cannot join | it

➡

2 it | shoes | is | in a living room | fine | for Americans | to wear

➡

3 very important | to exercise | it | regularly | is

➡

4 efficiency | makes | this machine | possible | to increase | it

➡

5 made | for them | it | difficult | the weather | to stay warm

➡

잘 모르겠다면 … 27페이지로

D 다음 ❶~❹의 우리말 뜻을 적으시오.

❶ It is a good idea to choose something interesting.
❷ Andy found it almost impossible to fix the computer.
❸ It is difficult to do your homework without any help.
❹ It was difficult for the boy to hear the whistle.

1

2

3

4

혼공기초

He / became interested
in dinosaurs.
그는 / 공룡에 관심을 가지게 되었다

혼공개념 001

주어에 대해 더 자세한 정보를 주는 것을 보어(**C**)라 하며 형용사, 명사, 동명사, **to** 부정사, 명사절 같이 다양한 것들이 와요. 주로 **be**동사와 감각 동사 뒤에 자주 쓰인답니다.

My goal is to help all dogs in this community.

This tomato soup tastes sweet.

The important thing is that he knows the truth.

The question is whether people will love this product.

목적어의 상태, 동작 등을 나타내는 것을 목적보어(**O.C.**)라고 해요. 형용사, 명사 외에도 다양한 준동사가 쓰인답니다.

We made Tommy angry.

They named their first child Sally.

Mr. Park allowed Jerry to go home early.

I saw him crossing the street.

개념확인문제 001   다음 우리말에 맞게 영작한 것을 고르시오.

1 그는 공룡에 관심을 가지게 되었다.

① He interested became in dinosaurs.
② He became interested in dinosaurs.

2 이 토마토 수프는 단맛이 난다.

① This tomato soup tastes sweet.
② This tomato soup tastes sweetly.

3 그들은 그들의 첫번째 아이를 Sally라고 이름지었다.

① They named Sally their first child.
② They named their first child Sally.

개념확인문제 002   다음 우리말에 맞게 순서를 바로잡아 영작하시오.

to go home / early / allowed / Mr. Park / Jerry	Park 선생님은 Jerry가 일찍 집에 가는 것을 허락하셨다.

A 다음 문장에서 밑줄 친 부분을 알맞게 해석하시오.

> 보기
> This mission <u>turned out impossible</u>.
> 불가능한 것으로 드러났다

(1) The first action <u>was moving slowly</u>.

_____

(2) Losing <u>isn't always a bad thing</u>.

_____

(3) Her voice <u>sounded strange on the phone</u>.

_____

B 괄호 안의 단어들을 순서에 맞게 써서 문장을 완성하시오.

(1) This (our | healthy | bones | keeps).

➡ This _____ .

(2) We (singing | him | saw | in the rain).

➡ We _____ .

(3) I (something | on my body | felt | crawling).

➡ I _____ .

C 다음 문장을 우리말로 해석하시오.

(1) His goal / is to learn something new.

➡

(2) It will make / the neighborhood a brighter place.

➡

32

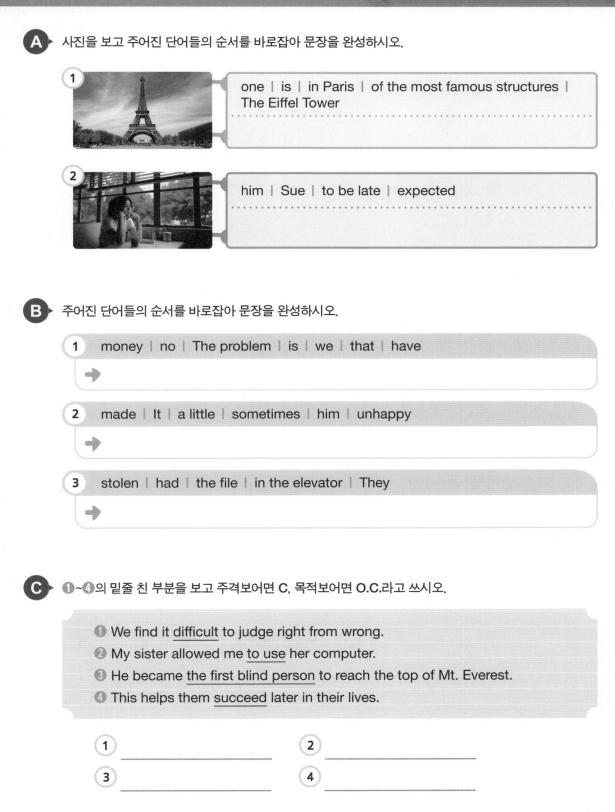

A 사진을 보고 주어진 단어들의 순서를 바로잡아 문장을 완성하시오.

1
one | is | in Paris | of the most famous structures | The Eiffel Tower
....

2
him | Sue | to be late | expected
....

B 주어진 단어들의 순서를 바로잡아 문장을 완성하시오.

1 money | no | The problem | is | we | that | have
➡

2 made | It | a little | sometimes | him | unhappy
➡

3 stolen | had | the file | in the elevator | They
➡

C ❶~❹의 밑줄 친 부분을 보고 주격보어면 C, 목적보어면 O.C.라고 쓰시오.

❶ We find it <u>difficult</u> to judge right from wrong.
❷ My sister allowed me <u>to use</u> her computer.
❸ He became <u>the first blind person</u> to reach the top of Mt. Everest.
❹ This helps them <u>succeed</u> later in their lives.

1 _____ **2** _____
3 _____ **4** _____

A 우리말 의미를 참고하여 빈칸을 알맞게 채우시오.

Q 잘 모르겠다면 ⋯→ 31페이지로

(1) 그는 공룡에 관심을 가지게 되었다.

He became [   ] in [   ] .

(2) 이 토마토 수프는 단맛이 난다.

This tomato [   ] [   ] sweet.

(3) 그들은 그들의 첫번째 아이를 Sally라고 이름지었다.

They [   ] their first [   ] Sally.

(4) Park 선생님은 Jerry가 일찍 집에 가는 것을 허락하셨다.

Mr. Park [   ] Jerry to [   ] home early.

B 다음 우리말에 맞게 순서를 바로잡아 영작하시오.

Q 잘 모르겠다면 ⋯→ 32페이지로

1 이 임무는 불가능한 것으로 드러났다.
mission | this | impossible | turned out

➡

2 그녀의 목소리는 전화상에서 이상하게 들렸다.
voice | on the phone | sounded | strange | her

➡

3 우리는 그가 빗속에서 노래부르는 것을 보았다.
singing | him | saw | we | in the rain

➡

4 그것은 이웃을 더 밝은 곳으로 만들 것이다.
will | it | make | a brighter place | the neighborhood

➡

C 주어진 단어들의 순서를 바로잡아 문장을 완성하시오. 🔍 잘 모르겠다면 …→ 33페이지로

1 one | is | in Paris | of the most famous structures | the Eiffel Tower

➡

2 him | Sue | to be late | expected

➡

3 money | no | the problem | is | we | that | have

➡

4 made | it | a little | sometimes | him | unhappy

➡

5 stolen | had | the file | in the elevator | they

➡

D 다음 ❶~❹의 우리말 뜻을 적으시오. 🔍 잘 모르겠다면 …→ 33페이지로

❶ We find it difficult to judge right from wrong.

❷ My sister allowed me to use her computer.

❸ He became the first blind person to reach the top of Mt. Everest.

❹ This helps them succeed later in their lives.

1

2

3

4

Part 2

동사의 확장
준동사

to 부정사의 명사적 용법/동명사

혼공기초

I began / to climb
the mountain.
나는 시작했다 / 그 산에 오르는 것을

혼공개념
001

'**to** + 동사원형'의 형태로 쓰는 것을 **to** 부정사라고 해요. 명사적 용법은 '~하기, ~하는 것'으로 해석하고 주어, 목적어, 보어 등의 자리에 와요. 특히 '의문사 + **to** 부정사'로 쓰이는 경우에도 해석 요령은 같으니 참고하세요.

To ask the right questions will help you a lot.

After the death of Socrates, Plato decided to travel abroad.

Another benefit is to save money.

To learn how to love myself was a new process.

동사를 **v-ing**로 쓰며 '~하는 것, ~하기'로 해석하는 것을 동명사라고 하고, **to** 부정사의 명사적 용법과 비슷한 자리에서 쓰여요. 하지만 **enjoy**, **practice**, **avoid**, **quit**, **mind**, **finish** 다음에는 **to** 부정사가 아닌 동명사가 반드시 와야 한답니다.

Traveling gives you new pleasures.

My hobby was collecting basketball cards.

Would you mind sharing the recipe?

Do you enjoy watching horror movies?

개념확인문제 001 다음 우리말에 맞게 영작한 것을 고르시오.

1 나는 그 산에 오르는 것을 시작했다.

① I began climb the mountain.
② I began to climb the mountain.

2 내 자신을 어떻게 사랑하는지를 배우는 것은 새로운 과정이었다.

① To learn how loving myself was a new process.
② To learn how to love myself was a new process.

3 그 요리법을 공유해주실 수 있으세요?

① Would you mind sharing the recipe?
② Would you mind to share the recipe?

개념확인문제 002 다음 우리말에 맞게 순서를 바로잡아 영작하시오.

| horror movies / you / Do / enjoy / watching | 너는 공포 영화를 시청하는 것을 즐기니? |

A 다음 문장에서 밑줄 친 부분을 알맞게 해석하시오.

> 보기
> She avoided <u>answering the questions</u>.
> 그 질문들에 답하는 것을

1 My goal <u>is to help all dogs</u> in this community.

_____

2 They need <u>to move to warmer and safer places</u>.

_____

3 The students <u>didn't finish studying</u> until the evening.

_____

B 괄호 안의 단어들을 순서에 맞게 써서 문장을 완성하시오.

1 My (the grass | thing | to lie | on | is | favorite).

➡ My _____ .

2 They (expected | in the morning | shopping | to go | early).

➡ They _____ .

3 I (wear | a uniform | want | don't | to).

➡ I _____ .

C 다음 문장을 우리말로 해석하시오.

1 You may not want / to go fishing with your father.

➡

2 Thinking positively / could help / you deal with stress.

➡

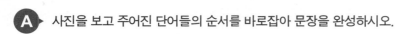

A ▶ 사진을 보고 주어진 단어들의 순서를 바로잡아 문장을 완성하시오.

1

for children | breakfast | is | Having | very important

....

2

to describe | of different candies | job | is | His | the flavor

....

B ▶ 주어진 단어들의 순서를 바로잡아 문장을 완성하시오.

1 for | is | vegetables | good | your health | Eating

➡

2 interview | helpful | questions | is | Practicing

➡

3 a seat belt | is | To wear | by law | required

➡

C ▶ ❶~❹의 괄호 안에서 어법상 알맞은 것을 골라 아래에 쓰시오.

❶ He decided to stop [using / use] it.

❷ I promised [going / to go] to the movies with Chris tonight.

❸ What do you plan [doing / to do] this weekend?

❹ Many people choose [having / to have] a pet these days.

1 _____ 2 _____ 3 _____ 4 _____

A 우리말 의미를 참고하여 빈칸을 알맞게 채우시오.

🔍 잘 모르겠다면 …▸ 39페이지로

(1) 나는 그 산에 오르는 것을 시작했다.

I _____ to _____ the mountain.

(2) 내 자신을 어떻게 사랑하는지를 배우는 것은 새로운 과정이었다.

To _____ how to love _____ was a new process.

(3) 그 요리법을 공유해주실 수 있으세요?

Would you _____ sharing the _____ ?

(4) 너는 공포 영화를 시청하는 것을 즐기니?

Do you _____ _____ horror movies?

B 다음 우리말에 맞게 순서를 바로잡아 영작하시오.

🔍 잘 모르겠다면 …▸ 40페이지로

1 그녀는 그 질문들에 답하는 것을 피했다.
avoided | she | the questions | answering
➡

2 내가 가장 좋아하는 것은 풀밭에 눕는 것이다.
the grass | thing | to lie | my | on | is | favorite
➡

3 너는 너의 아버지와 낚시하러 가는 것을 아마 원하지 않을 것이다.
want | fishing | your father | you | to go | with | may not
➡

4 긍정적으로 생각하는 것은 네가 스트레스를 다루는데 도움이 될 수 있다.
help | positively | stress | could | thinking | you | deal with
➡

C 주어진 단어들의 순서를 바로잡아 문장을 완성하시오.

잘 모르겠다면 ..., 41페이지로

1 for children | breakfast | is | having | very important

➡

2 to describe | of different candies | job | is | his | the flavor

➡

3 for | is | vegetables | good | your health | eating

➡

4 interview | helpful | questions | is | practicing

➡

5 a seat belt | is | to wear | by law | required

➡

D 다음 ❶~❹의 우리말 뜻을 적으시오.

잘 모르겠다면 ..., 41페이지로

❶ He decided to stop using it.
❷ I promised to go to the movies with Chris tonight.
❸ What do you plan to do this weekend?
❹ Many people choose to have a pet these days.

1 _____

2 _____

3 _____

4 _____

to 부정사의 형용사적 용법

혼공기초

**A gondola ride is an amazing way /
to see Venice.**

곤돌라 타기는 놀라운 방법이다 /
Venice를 보는

**혼공개념
001**

to 부정사가 명사 뒤에서 형용사 처럼 '~하는, ~할'이라고 해석되는 것을 형용사적 용법이라고 해요.

They needed something to drink.

Getting enough sleep is one way to stay healthy.

The best way to do this is to take your time.

The young guy had a desire to buy the car.

to 부정사의 형용사적 용법에는 전치사가 따라오는 경우가 있어요. 앞에 있는 명사를 그 뒤에 위치시켜 보면 전치사가 필요한지를 확인할 수 있답니다.

They have no house to live in.

The police officer was looking for something to write with.

I need a friend to talk to.

There is no field for Rocky to exercise in.

개념확인문제 001 다음 우리말에 맞게 영작한 것을 고르시오.

1 곤돌라 타기는 Venice를 보는 놀라운 방법이다.

① A gondola ride is an amazing way see Venice.
② A gondola ride is an amazing way to see Venice.

2 그들은 마실 어떤 것이 필요했다.

① They needed something to drink.
② They needed to drink something.

3 그들은 살 집이 없다.

① They have no house to live.
② They have no house to live in.

개념확인문제 002 다음 우리말에 맞게 순서를 바로잡아 영작하시오.

to write with / something / was / The police officer / looking for	그 경찰관은 쓸 어떤 것을 찾고 있는 중이었다.

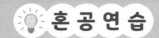

A 다음 문장에서 밑줄 친 부분을 알맞게 해석하시오.

> 보기 Some office workers have <u>many interesting things to do after work.</u>
> <u>퇴근 후에 할 많은 흥미로운 것들을</u>

1 The Internet <u>is a great way to communicate with each other.</u>

   _____

2 Gyeongju has <u>a lot of historical sites to visit.</u>

   _____

3 They <u>don't have a car to drive.</u>

   _____

B 괄호 안의 단어들을 순서에 맞게 써서 문장을 완성하시오.

1 She (has | us | our happiness | ideas | to improve | given)

   ➡ She _____ .

2 They (solve | had some | to | problems)

   ➡ They _____ .

3 I (you | something | to tell | have)

   ➡ I _____ .

C 다음 문장을 우리말로 해석하시오.

1 The best way to overcome shyness / is to have confidence.

   ➡

2 They have the potential / to become good friends.

   ➡

46

🎯 혼공완성

A 사진을 보고 주어진 단어들의 순서를 바로잡아 문장을 완성하시오.

1

the theory | There | to test | a few | are | reasons

....

2

A good park | dogs | would | a great way | healthy | to keep | be

....

B 주어진 단어들의 순서를 바로잡아 문장을 완성하시오.

1 goodbye | is | to | the time | to say | everyone | Tomorrow

➡

2 spend | needs some | Anna | money | to

➡

3 to save | These | are | the environment | great ways

➡

C ❶~❹의 빈칸을 알맞은 전치사로 채우시오.

❶ Mom gave me a sheet of paper to write _____.

❷ We have no chair to sit _____.

❸ This is the topic to talk _____.

❹ Mike has a lot of friends to play _____.

① _____   ② _____   ③ _____   ④ _____

혼공복습

A 우리말 의미를 참고하여 빈칸을 알맞게 채우시오.

🔍 잘 모르겠다면 ···→ 45페이지로

(1) 곤돌라 타기는 Venice를 보는 놀라운 방법이다.

A gondola ride is an ⬜⬜⬜ way ⬜⬜⬜ see Venice.

(2) 그들은 마실 어떤 것이 필요했다.

They ⬜⬜⬜ something to ⬜⬜⬜ .

(3) 그들은 살 집이 없다.

They have no ⬜⬜⬜ to ⬜⬜⬜ in.

(4) 그 경찰관은 쓸 어떤 것(필기구)을 찾고 있는 중이었다.

The police officer was ⬜⬜⬜ for something to write ⬜⬜⬜ .

B 다음 우리말에 맞게 순서를 바로잡아 영작하시오.

🔍 잘 모르겠다면 ···→ 46페이지로

(1) 그들은 운전할 차를 가지고 있지 않다.
don't | a car | to | have | drive | they

➡

(2) 그녀는 우리의 행복을 향상시킬 아이디어를 우리들에게 주었다.
has | us | our happiness | she | ideas | to improve | given

➡

(3) 부끄러움을 극복하는 최선의 방법은 자신감을 갖는 것이다.
way | confidence | shyness | is | to have | to overcome | the best

➡

(4) 그들은 좋은 친구가 될 잠재력을 가지고 있다.
the potential | become | have | to | good friends | they

➡

C 주어진 단어들의 순서를 바로잡아 문장을 완성하시오.

🔍 잘 모르겠다면 ..., 47페이지로

1 the theory | there | to test | a few | are | reasons

➡

2 a good park | dogs | would | a great way | healthy | to keep | be

➡

3 goodbye | is | to | the time | to say | everyone | tomorrow

➡

4 spend | needs some | Anna | money | to

➡

5 to save | these | are | the environment | great ways

➡

D 다음 ❶~❹의 우리말 뜻을 적으시오.

🔍 잘 모르겠다면 ..., 47페이지로

❶ Mom gave me a sheet of paper to write on.
❷ We have no chair to sit on.
❸ This is the topic to talk about.
❹ Mike has a lot of friends to play with.

1

2

3

4

to 부정사의 부사적 용법

혼공기초

A few volcano scientists were there / to warn the people.

몇몇 화산 과학자들은 거기에 있었다 / 사람들에게 경고하기 위해서

혼공개념 001

to 부정사의 부사적 용법은 아주 다양한 해석이 있어요. 그 중에서 대표적인 것이 목적(~하기 위해), 감정의 원인(~해서)이 있어요. 또한 문장 앞이나 중간, 끝에서 문장 전체를 수식하기도 해요.

People sing **to work** together effectively. 목적

You should jump rope **to make** your legs strong. 목적

He was happy **to see** her smile. 감정의 원인

To tell the truth, my car has broken down. 문장 전체

'그 결과 ~했다'라는 의미의 결과도 부사적 용법의 한 종류이지요.
'너무 ~해서 ~할 수 없다'라는 의미의 '**too ~ to**' 용법과 '~하기에 충분히 ~
한'이라는 '**enough to**' 용법도 같이 알아두세요.

He grew up to be a great doctor. 결과

I left home early only to miss the flight. 결과

The chair is too big to carry on my own. too ~ to

The kid was smart enough to break the code. enough to

개념확인문제 001 다음 우리말에 맞게 영작한 것을 고르시오.

1 몇몇 화산 과학자들은 사람들에게 경고하기 위해서 거기에 있었다.

① A few volcano scientists were there warn the people.
② A few volcano scientists were there to warn the people.

2 그는 그녀의 미소를 봐서 행복했다.

① He was happy see her smile.
② He was happy to see her smile.

3 그는 자라서 대단한 의사가 되었다.

① He grew up to be a great doctor.
② He grew up being a great doctor.

개념확인문제 002 다음 우리말에 맞게 순서를 바로잡아 영작하시오.

| on my own / is / too / to carry / big / The chair | 그 의자는 너무 커서 내 스스로 운반할 수 없다. |

 혼공연습

A 다음 문장에서 밑줄 친 부분을 알맞게 해석하시오.

> 보기
>
> She ran after the bus <u>to get her umbrella back</u>.
> <u>그녀의 우산을 다시 찾기 위해서</u>

(1) We are writing <u>to remind you about his birthday</u>.

_____

(2) What should I do <u>to make things better</u>?

_____

(3) <u>To make matters worse</u>, it began to rain.

_____

B 괄호 안의 단어들을 순서에 맞게 써서 문장을 완성하시오.

(1) I (my wife | the window | not | closed | to disturb).

→ I _____ .

(2) You (to stay | about | 40 | need | nutrients | different | healthy).

→ You _____ .

(3) She (to raise | of birds | paintings | money | made).

→ She _____ .

C 다음 문장을 우리말로 해석하시오.

(1) This new model is small enough / to fit in a pocket.

→

(2) Her parents were shocked / to find out she quit school.

→

혼공완성

A 사진을 보고 주어진 단어들의 순서를 바로잡아 문장을 완성하시오.

1

are | to eat | too | sweet | every day | Macarons

....

2

to celebrate | is | Dance | often | used |
an important event

....

B 주어진 단어들의 순서를 바로잡아 문장을 완성하시오.

1 impossible | Dishonesty | to | hide | is

➡

2 wake up | quickly | Most | to take care of | parents | their babies

➡

3 use | dance | express | to | People | themselves

➡

C ❶~❹의 밑줄 친 부분에 해당되는 to 부정사의 부사적 용법을 '목적, 결과, 감정의 원인, 문장 전체 수식' 중 골라서 빈칸에 쓰시오.

❶ To get these necessary nutrients, you must balance your food choices.
❷ James was very pleased to see him again.
❸ To be sure, K-pop is becoming popular around the world.
❹ My grandparents lived to be eighty.

1 _____ 2 _____ 3 _____ 4 _____

A 우리말 의미를 참고하여 빈칸을 알맞게 채우시오.

잘 모르겠다면 ···› 51페이지로

(1) 몇몇 화산 과학자들은 사람들에게 경고하기 위해서 거기에 있었다.

A few _____ scientists were there to _____ the people.

(2) 그는 그녀의 미소를 봐서 행복했다.

He was _____ to _____ her smile.

(3) 그는 자라서 대단한 의사가 되었다.

He _____ up to _____ a great doctor.

(4) 그 의자는 너무 커서 내 스스로 운반할 수 없다.

The chair is _____ big to _____ on my own.

B 다음 우리말에 맞게 순서를 바로잡아 영작하시오.

잘 모르겠다면 ···› 52페이지로

(1) 그녀는 그녀의 우산을 다시 찾기 위해서 그 버스를 쫓아 달려갔다.
to get | ran after | her umbrella | the bus | back | she

➡

(2) 나는 내 와이프를 방해하지 않기 위해서 창문을 닫았다.
my wife | the window | not | I | closed | to disturb

➡

(3) 이 새로운 모델은 주머니에 딱 들어갈 만큼 충분히 작다.
new | in a pocket | small | model | is | enough | this | to fit

➡

(4) 그녀의 부모님은 그녀가 학교를 그만두었다는 것을 알고 충격받았다.
were | school | shocked | to find out | parents | she | her | quit

➡

잘 모르겠다면 ⋯› 53페이지로

C 주어진 단어들의 순서를 바로잡아 문장을 완성하시오.

1 are | to eat | too | sweet | every day | macarons

➡

2 to celebrate | is | dance | often | used | an important event

➡

3 impossible | dishonesty | to | hide | is

➡

4 wake up | quickly | most | to take care of | parents | their babies

➡

5 use | dance | express | to | people | themselves

➡

잘 모르겠다면 ⋯› 53페이지로

D 다음 ❶~❹의 우리말 뜻을 적으시오.

❶ To get these necessary nutrients, you must balance your food choices.

❷ James was very pleased to see him again.

❸ To be sure, K-pop is becoming popular around the world.

❹ My grandparents lived to be eighty.

1 _____

2 _____

3 _____

4 _____

to 부정사의 be to 용법

혼공기초

This couple / is to get married in January.
이 커플은 / 1월에 결혼할 것이다

혼공개념
001

be 동사 다음에 **to** 부정사가 오는 경우 조동사의 의미를 살린 예정(~할 것이다), 의무(~해야 한다), 가능(~할 수 있다)의 의미로 해석이 된답니다. **to** 부정사의 명사적 용법(~하기, ~하는 것)과 해석 차이가 있으니 반드시 문맥을 고려해야 해요.

The championships are to be held **in Rome.**

She is to clean **the room by five.**

No one was to be seen **in the town.**

Another benefit is to save **money.** 명사적 용법

if절 안에서 **be to**용법이 쓰인다면 의도(~한다면)의 의미이고, 드물지만 운명(~할 운명이다)으로 해석되기도 해요.

If **trees** are to grow **well**, there are some things to be cut off.

Good nutrition is essential if **patients** are to make **a quick recovery.**

Bruno Mars **was to be** a superstar.

They **are to be** together forever.

개념확인문제　001　다음 우리말에 맞게 영작한 것을 고르시오.

1 이 커플은 1월에 결혼할 것이다.

① This couple is get married in January.
② This couple is to get married in January.

2 그녀는 방을 5시까지 청소해야 한다.

① She is to clean the room by five.
② She to clean is the room by five.

3 Bruno Mars는 슈퍼스타가 될 운명이었다.

① Bruno Mars is to be a superstar.
② Bruno Mars was to be a superstar.

개념확인문제　002　다음 우리말에 맞게 순서를 바로잡아 영작하시오.

| to / was / seen / be / in the town / No one | 아무도 마을에서 볼 수 없었다. |

 다음 문장에서 밑줄 친 부분을 알맞게 해석하시오.

> **보기**
> Students <u>are to do their homework</u> every day.
> 그들의 숙제를 해야 한다

1 They <u>are to succeed</u> with her assistance.

_____

2 The president <u>is to attend an international conference</u> next month.

_____

3 <u>If we are to succeed</u>, we should keep learning forever.

_____

B 괄호 안의 단어들을 순서에 맞게 써서 문장을 완성하시오.

1 You (this | a mask | in | to wear | operating room | are).

➡ You _____ .

2 The chef (the cooking festival | is | to | New York | visit | for).

➡ The chef _____ .

3 She (by midnight | to | to | go back | is | her home).

➡ She _____ .

C 다음 문장을 우리말로 해석하시오.

1 Nothing / was to be found.

➡

2 All people / are to die someday.

➡

58

A 사진을 보고 주어진 단어들의 순서를 바로잡아 문장을 완성하시오.

1
depart | The next train | three o'clock | is | at | to

....

2
the hurricane | is | The exam | delayed | to be |
because of

....

B 주어진 단어들의 순서를 바로잡아 문장을 완성하시오.

1 wash | People | to | are | hands | their

➡

2 become | to | a | He | is | scientist | great

➡

3 next year | to | be | The Olympic Games | are | held

➡

C 우리말 힌트를 참고하여 ❶~❹의 빈칸을 알맞게 채우시오.

❶ The chairman is _____ Paris for the meeting. (떠나다)
❷ They are _____ until next year to use that bridge. (기다리다)
❸ Gardeners are _____ it more water to make it bloom. (주다)
❹ You are not _____ any instruments in the laboratory. (만지다)

1 _____ 2 _____ 3 _____ 4 _____

혼공복습

A 우리말 의미를 참고하여 빈칸을 알맞게 채우시오.

🔍 잘 모르겠다면 …→ 57페이지로

(1) 이 커플은 1월에 결혼할 것이다.

This _____ is to get _____ in January.

(2) 그녀는 방을 5시까지 청소해야 한다.

She is to _____ the _____ by five.

(3) Bruno Mars는 슈퍼스타가 될 운명이었다.

Bruno Mars _____ to _____ a superstar.

(4) 아무도 마을에서 볼 수 없었다.

No _____ was to be _____ in the town.

B 다음 우리말에 맞게 순서를 바로잡아 영작하시오.

🔍 잘 모르겠다면 …→ 58페이지로

1 대통령은 다음 달 국제 회의에 참가할 것이다.
is | next month | an international conference | to attend | the president

➡

2 당신은 이 수술실에서 마스크를 착용해야 한다.
this | a mask | in | to wear | you | operating room | are

➡

3 그녀는 자정까지 그녀의 집으로 돌아가야 한다.
by midnight | to | to | she | go back | is | her home

➡

4 아무것도 발견할 수 없었다.
nothing | found | was | be | to

➡

C 주어진 단어들의 순서를 바로잡아 문장을 완성하시오.

잘 모르겠다면 ···▸ 59페이지로

1 depart | the next train | three o'clock | is | at | to

➡

2 the hurricane | is | the exam | delayed | to be | because of

➡

3 wash | people | to | are | hands | their

➡

4 become | to | a | he | is | scientist | great

➡

5 next year | to | be | the Olympic Games | are | held

➡

D 다음 ❶~❹의 우리말 뜻을 적으시오.

잘 모르겠다면 ···▸ 59페이지로

❶ The chairman is to leave Paris for the meeting.

❷ They are to wait until next year to use that bridge.

❸ Gardeners are to give it more water to make it bloom.

❹ You are not to touch any instruments in the laboratory.

① _____

② _____

③ _____

④ _____

혼공기초

**My mother told me /
an interesting story.**
내 어머니께서 나에게 말해주셨다 /
한 흥미로운 이야기를

혼공개념
001

동사를 빌려와서 형용사로 만들어 쓰는 것을 분사라고 해요. 그 중 현재분사는
'**v-ing**'의 형태로 '~하게 하는, ~하는 중인'의 의미로 쓰여요. 명사를 수식하는
역할을 하기도 하고, **be**동사 다음에 쓰여서 진행형을 나타내기도 하지요.

He quit the boring job to go to New York.

The experience in the park was totally satisfying.

A kid was crying after school.

She saw her father standing there.

과거분사(p.p.)는 'v-ed' 또는 불규칙 형태로 쓰이며 '~해진, 되어진'의 의미로 쓰여요. 명사를 수식하는 역할을 하기도 하고, 수동태, 완료시제에 꼭 필요한 단어에요.

Earth's largest recorded earthquake struck Chile.

It made us feel confused about math.

The boss had the computer repaired.

The tower was constructed using 18,000 pieces of iron.

개념확인문제 001 다음 우리말에 맞게 영작한 것을 고르시오.

1 내 어머니께서 한 흥미로운 이야기를 나에게 말해주셨다.

① My mother told me an interested story.
② My mother told me an interesting story.

2 그는 New York에 가기 위해 지겨운 직장을 그만두었다.

① He quit the bored job to go to New York.
② He quit the boring job to go to New York.

3 그것은 우리들이 수학에 대해 혼란을 느끼도록 했다.

① It made us feel confused about math.
② It made us feel confusing about math.

개념확인문제 002 다음 우리말에 맞게 순서를 바로잡아 영작하시오.

recorded / largest / earthquake / struck / Earth's / Chile	지구상에서 가장 큰 것으로 기록된 지진이 칠레를 강타했다.

➡

 혼공연습

 다음 문장에서 밑줄 친 부분을 알맞게 해석하시오.

> 보기
>
> My brother left this cake untouched.
> 이 케익을 만지지 않은 채로 두었다

(1) The movie theater next to the school is always crowded.

_____

(2) Millionaires were invited to buy islands named after countries.

_____

(3) The idea of living underwater is too frightening to think about.

_____

B 괄호 안의 단어들을 순서에 맞게 써서 문장을 완성하시오.

(1) She (called | her | heard | name).

➡ She   .

(2) I (the amazing views | at night | enjoyed | of the city).

➡ I   .

(3) Olivia (the damage | heard | caused | by | about | the oil spill).

➡ Olivia   .

C 다음 문장을 우리말로 해석하시오.

(1) The criminal tried to avoid / an embarrassing question.

➡

(2) There was a monkey / sitting on a rock.

➡

혼공완성

A 사진을 보고 주어진 단어들의 순서를 바로잡아 문장을 완성하시오.

①

a fast wave | This | called | creates | a tsunami

....

②

that | Doctors | is | say | the key | variety |
to a balanced diet

....

B 주어진 단어들의 순서를 바로잡아 문장을 완성하시오.

① My | over a parked car | son | tried | 13-year-old | to jump

➡

② her | saw | She | standing | neighbor | there

➡

③ have | The coins | of nature's wonders | ruined | one

➡

C ①~④의 괄호 안에서 어법상 알맞은 것을 골라 아래에 쓰시오.

❶ An hour before the performance, I got [dressing / dressed].
❷ This was actually the [expecting / expected] result.
❸ They can hear the frogs [singing / sung] in the ponds nearby.
❹ This movie looks [exciting / excited] and fun.

① _____   ② _____   ③ _____   ④ _____

혼공복습

A 우리말 의미를 참고하여 빈칸을 알맞게 채우시오.

잘 모르겠다면 …→ 63페이지로

1. 내 어머니께서 한 흥미로운 이야기를 나에게 말해주셨다.

   My mother _____ me an _____ story.

2. 그는 New York에 가기 위해 지겨운 직장을 그만두었다.

   He _____ the _____ job to go to New York.

3. 그것은 우리들이 수학에 대해 혼란을 느끼도록 했다.

   It made us feel _____ about _____.

4. 지구상에서 가장 큰 것으로 기록된 지진이 칠레를 강타했다.

   Earth's largest _____ earthquake _____ Chile.

B 다음 우리말에 맞게 순서를 바로잡아 영작하시오.

잘 모르겠다면 …→ 64페이지로

1. 그 학교 옆에 있는 영화 극장은 항상 사람으로 붐빈다.
   next to | the school | the movie theater | is | crowded | always

   ➡

2. 그녀는 그녀의 이름이 불리는 것을 들었다.
   called | her | she | heard | name

   ➡

3. 그 범죄자는 당황스러운 질문을 피하려고 노력했다.
   tried | an embarrassing | to avoid | the criminal | question

   ➡

4. 바위에 앉아 있는 원숭이가 한 마리 있었다.
   was | there | a monkey | on a rock | sitting

   ➡

잘 모르겠다면 ..., 65페이지로

C 주어진 단어들의 순서를 바로잡아 문장을 완성하시오.

1 a fast wave | this | called | creates | a tsunami

➡

2 that | doctors | is | say | the key | variety | to a balanced diet

➡

3 my | over a parked car | son | tried | 13-year-old | to jump

➡

4 her | saw | she | standing | neighbor | there

➡

5 have | the coins | of nature's wonders | ruined | one

➡

D 다음 ❶~❹의 우리말 뜻을 적으시오.

잘 모르겠다면 ..., 65페이지로

❶ An hour before the performance, I got dressed.

❷ This was actually the expected result.

❸ They can hear the frogs singing in the ponds nearby.

❹ This movie looks exciting and fun.

1

2

3

4

분사구문

혼공기초

**Dressed in pink, /
she looked like a rose.**

분홍색으로 옷을 입어서, /
그녀는 장미처럼 보였다

**혼공개념
001**

문장 주위에 있는 현재분사 또는 과거분사가 쓰인 어구를 분사구문이라고 해요. 주어와 접속사가 생략된 경우가 대부분이라, 근처에 있는 주어를 떠올리면서 시간(~때, ~동안에), 이유(~때문에), 조건(~한다면), 양보(~에도 불구하고)의 접속사를 살려서 해석하면 된답니다.

Boiling eggs, I burned my hand badly.

Arriving at the party, we saw her standing alone.

Being away from her family, she felt lonely.

**Going down the hall, you will find
the restroom on your left.**

분사구문을 부정할 때는 분사 앞에 **not**을 써요. 그리고 분사구문이 쓰인 부분의 시제가 다음 문장의 시제보다 앞설 때는 **having p.p.**를 쓴답니다. **(Being) p.p.** ~로 시작되는 분사구문은 **Being**을 생략한 형태로 종종 쓰고, **having been**도 생략할수 있어요.

Not knowing what to say, he kept silent.

Having done her homework, she has nothing to do now.

Based on this idea, Lauren Brent spent four years researching.

Left alone at the zoo, the boy started to cry.

개념확인문제 001 다음 우리말에 맞게 영작한 것을 고르시오.

1 분홍색으로 옷을 입어서, 그녀는 장미처럼 보였다.

① Dressed in pink, she looked like a rose.
② Dressing in pink, she looked like a rose.

2 뭐라고 말할지 몰라서, 그는 침묵을 지켰다.

① Knowing not to say what, he kept silent.
② Not knowing what to say, he kept silent.

3 그녀의 숙제를 했기 때문에, 그녀는 지금 할 것이 없다.

① Done her homework, she has nothing to do now.
② Having done her homework, she has nothing to do now.

개념확인문제 002 다음 우리말에 맞게 순서를 바로잡아 영작하시오.

| the boy / alone / to cry / Left / at the zoo / started | 동물원에 혼자 남겨져서, 그 소년은 울기 시작했다. |

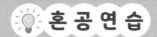

 다음 문장에서 밑줄 친 부분을 알맞게 해석하시오.

> 보기
> <u>Taking a shower</u>, he always has the radio on.
> 샤워를 할 때(동안에)

1 <u>Living in France</u>, she speaks French fluently.

_____

2 <u>Feeling tired</u>, I went to bed early.

_____

3 <u>Opening the drawer</u>, she found a secret diary.

_____

 괄호 안의 것을 의미에 맞게 순서대로 쓰시오.

1 (his | knowing | Not | number), I couldn't call him.

➡

2 (to | the news | hear | Excited), he went straight to his wife.

➡

3 (the movie | on TV | seen | Having | recently), I didn't want to see it again.

➡

 다음 문장을 우리말로 해석하시오.

1 Having little money, / she couldn't afford a new car.

➡

2 Not wanting to be late, / I took a taxi to school.

➡

A 우리말 해석과 주어진 동사를 활용하여 알맞은 분사구문을 쓰시오.

1
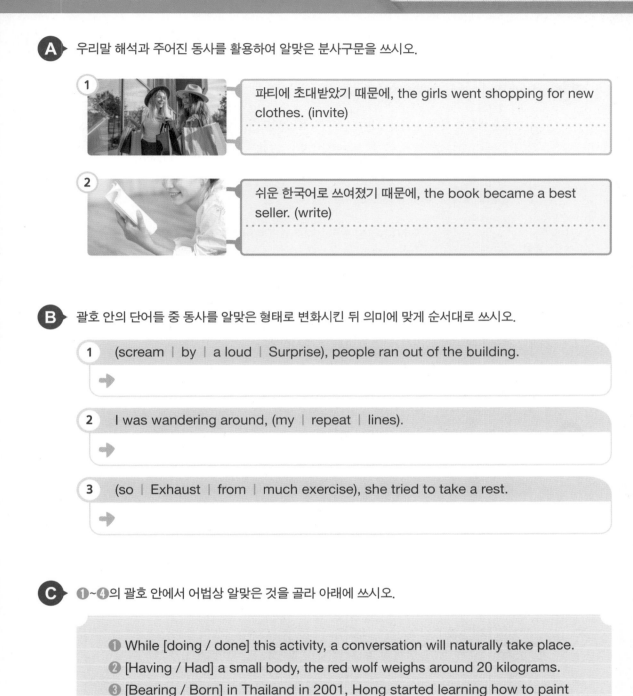
파티에 초대받았기 때문에, the girls went shopping for new clothes. (invite)
....

2
쉬운 한국어로 쓰여졌기 때문에, the book became a best seller. (write)
....

B 괄호 안의 단어들 중 동사를 알맞은 형태로 변화시킨 뒤 의미에 맞게 순서대로 쓰시오.

1 (scream | by | a loud | Surprise), people ran out of the building.

➡

2 I was wandering around, (my | repeat | lines).

➡

3 (so | Exhaust | from | much exercise), she tried to take a rest.

➡

C ❶~❹의 괄호 안에서 어법상 알맞은 것을 골라 아래에 쓰시오.

❶ While [doing / done] this activity, a conversation will naturally take place.

❷ [Having / Had] a small body, the red wolf weighs around 20 kilograms.

❸ [Bearing / Born] in Thailand in 2001, Hong started learning how to paint in 2005.

❹ [Bring / Brought] from the journey, the pretty glasses were displayed there.

① _____ ② _____ ③ _____ ④ _____

A 우리말 의미를 참고하여 빈칸을 알맞게 채우시오.

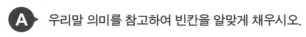 잘 모르겠다면 ⋯ 69페이지로

(1) 분홍색으로 옷을 입어서, 그녀는 장미처럼 보였다.

_____ in pink, she looked _____ a rose.

(2) 뭐라고 말할지 몰라서, 그는 침묵을 지켰다.

_____ knowing what to say, he kept _____ .

(3) 그녀의 숙제를 했기 때문에, 그녀는 지금 할 것이 없다.

_____ done her homework, she has _____ to do now.

(4) 동물원에 혼자 남겨져서, 그 소년은 울기 시작했다.

_____ alone at the zoo, the boy started to _____ .

B 다음 우리말에 맞게 순서를 바로잡아 영작하시오.

잘 모르겠다면 ⋯ 70페이지로

1 프랑스에 살기 때문에 그녀는 프랑스어를 유창하게 한다.
fluently | she | in France | living | French | speaks

➡

2 피곤해서, 나는 일찍 자러갔다.
I | went | tired | feeling | to bed | early

➡

3 그의 번호를 몰라서, 나는 그에게 전화할 수 없었다.
call | I | his | knowing | not | number | couldn't | him

➡

4 늦고 싶지 않았기 때문에, 나는 학교에 택시를 타고 갔다.
wanting | to school | to be | I | late | took | not | a taxi

➡

1 (to | the news | hear | excited), he went straight to his wife.

➡

2 (the movie | on TV | seen | having | recently), I didn't want to see it again.

➡

3 (easy | in | Korean | written), the book became a best seller.

➡

4 (scream | by | a loud | surprised), people ran out of the building.

➡

5 (so | exhausted | from | much exercise), she tried to take a rest.

➡

❶ While doing this activity, a conversation will naturally take place.
❷ Having a small body, the red wolf weighs around 20 kilograms.
❸ Born in Thailand in 2001, Hong started learning how to paint in 2005.
❹ Brought from the journey, the pretty glasses were displayed there.

1

2

3

4

문장의 확장 관계사

관계대명사 – 주격

혼공기초

**Do not ride a bike /
that is too big for you.**
자전거를 타지 마세요 / 당신에게 너무 큰

**혼공개념
001**

두 개의 문장을 합칠 때 관계대명사를 쓰는데, 생략된 단어가 주어 자리라면 주격관계대명사를 써요. 보통 관계대명사 앞에 있는 단어를 선행사라고 하는데, 선행사가 사람일 때는 관계대명사 **who**, **that**을 쓴답니다.

I know a man who lives across the street.

He is the one who wrote *The Old Man and the Sea*.

I know the girl who is wearing a red skirt.

**You can save the life of someone
who needs your help.**

선행사가 사물이거나 동물인 경우에는 주격관계대명사로 보통 **which**, **that**을 쓴답니다. 결국 선행사 종류 관계없이 **that**을 쓰면 편해요.

This is the picture that was taken last year.

Find a shampoo that is good for your hair.

This is a convenience store which is open 24 hours a day.

The cat which is sitting on the fence looks very scary.

개념확인문제 001 다음 우리말에 맞게 영작한 것을 고르시오.

1 당신에게 너무 큰 자전거를 타지 마세요.

① Do not ride a bike who is too big for you.
② Do not ride a bike that is too big for you.

2 나는 빨간색 치마를 입고 있는 그 소녀를 안다.

① I know the girl who is wearing a red skirt.
② I know the girl which is wearing a red skirt.

3 네 머리카락에 좋은 샴푸를 찾아라.

① Find a shampoo who is good for your hair.
② Find a shampoo that is good for your hair.

개념확인문제 002 다음 우리말에 맞게 순서를 바로잡아 영작하시오.

which / looks / on the fence / is sitting / very scary / The cat	담장 위에 앉아 있는 고양이는 아주 무서워 보인다.

A 다음 문장에서 밑줄 친 부분을 알맞게 해석하시오.

> 보기   My sister who lives in Canada is a biologist.
> 캐나다에 사는 내 여동생은

(1) I know a girl who is good at math.

_____

(2) He likes to read books that are very interesting.

_____

(3) You can eat the fruits that are on the table.

_____

B 괄호 안의 단어들을 순서에 맞게 써서 문장을 완성하시오.

(1) Tito is a businessman (always | wanted | who | had | to be | an astronaut).

➡ _____

(2) Look at the cute baby (is | who | sleeping | the bed | on).

➡ _____

(3) A teacher is a person (teaches | school | students | at | who).

➡ _____

C 다음 문장을 우리말로 해석하시오.

(1) Teens who have close relationships / with their family members / are lucky.

➡ _____

(2) People who live near schools / quickly learn not to drive fast.

➡ _____

A 사진을 보고 주어진 단어들의 순서를 바로잡아 문장을 완성하시오.

1

remember | the boy | a blue | I | wore | who | sweater

. . . .

2

successful | a shop | was | A man had | very | that

. . . .

B 주어진 단어들의 순서를 바로잡아 문장을 완성하시오.

1 met | hearing difficulties | He | who | a boy | had

2 at a little village school | was | a teacher | worked | who | Mr. Gordon

3 who | to you | at school | someone | can | Having | listens | really help

C 알맞은 관계대명사를 활용하여 다음 ❶과 ❷, ❸과 ❹를 각각 연결하시오.

❶ Each coin has blocked the small holes.
❷ They give the pool its heat.
❸ There once was a king.
❹ He was defeated in a battle.

(1) + (2) _____

(3) + (4) _____

A 우리말 의미를 참고하여 빈칸을 알맞게 채우시오. 🔍 잘 모르겠다면 ⋯ 77페이지로

(1) 당신에게 너무 큰 자전거를 타지 마세요.

Do not ⬚⬚⬚ a bike ⬚⬚⬚ is too big for you.

(2) 나는 빨간색 치마를 입고 있는 그 소녀를 안다.

I ⬚⬚⬚ the girl who is ⬚⬚⬚ a red skirt.

(3) 네 머리카락에 좋은 샴푸를 찾아라.

⬚⬚⬚ a shampoo that is good for your ⬚⬚⬚ .

(4) 담장 위에 앉아 있는 고양이는 아주 무서워 보인다.

The cat ⬚⬚⬚ is sitting on the fence ⬚⬚⬚ very scary.

B 다음 우리말에 맞게 순서를 바로잡아 영작하시오. 🔍 잘 모르겠다면 ⋯ 78페이지로

(1) 캐나다에 사는 내 여동생은 생물학자이다.
who | is | lives | my | in Canada | sister | a biologist
➡

(2) Tito는 항상 우주비행사가 되고 싶어 했던 사업가이다.
always | is | a businessman | wanted | who | Tito | had | to be | an astronaut
➡

(3) 침대에서 자고 있는 귀여운 아기를 봐라.
is | who | sleeping | the bed | the cute baby | look at | on
➡

(4) 교사는 학교에서 학생들을 가르치는 사람이다.
a person | teaches | school | is | students | at | a teacher | who
➡

C 주어진 단어들의 순서를 바로잡아 문장을 완성하시오. 🔍 잘 모르겠다면 ⋯ 79페이지로

1 remember | the boy | a blue | I | wore | who | sweater

➡

2 successful | a shop | was | a man had | very | that

➡

3 met | hearing difficulties | he | who | a boy | had

➡

4 at a little village school | was | a teacher | worked | who | Mr. Gordon

➡

5 who | to you | at school | someone | can | having | listens | really help

➡

D 다음 ❶~❹의 우리말 뜻을 적으시오. 🔍 잘 모르겠다면 ⋯ 79페이지로

❶ Each coin has blocked the small holes.
❷ They give the pool its heat.
❸ There once was a king.
❹ He was defeated in a battle.

1

2

3

4

관계대명사 – 목적격

혼공기초

**I love the flowers /
which he bought for me.**
나는 꽃들을 사랑한다 /
그가 나를 위해 사주었던

**혼공개념
001**

관계대명사를 쓰면서 두 문장을 합칠 때, 생략된 단어가 목적어 자리라면
목적격관계대명사를 써요. 선행사가 사람일 때는 관계대명사 **who**, **whom**,
that을 쓴답니다.

There is a girl who(m) I like in my class.

The singer is a famous K-pop star who(m) most teenagers like.

He is the doctor who(m) everyone respects.

**Who was the woman that I saw at
a concert hall?**

혼공개념 002

선행사가 사물이거나 동물인 경우에는 목적격관계대명사로 보통 **which**, **that**을 씁니다. 또한 주격관계대명사와 달리 목적격관계대명사는 생략이 가능해요.

This is the picture which I took last year.

The skirt that I bought last year doesn't fit me anymore.

At the party there were many people (whom) he did not know.

Soil stores the water (that) the crops need.

개념확인문제 001 다음 우리말에 맞게 영작한 것을 고르시오.

1 나는 그가 나를 위해 사주었던 꽃들을 사랑한다.

① I love the flowers who he bought for me.
② I love the flowers which he bought for me.

2 그 가수는 대부분의 십대들이 좋아하는 유명한 케이팝 스타이다.

① The singer is a famous K-pop star whom most teenagers like.
② The singer is a famous K-pop star which most teenagers like.

3 내가 작년에 샀던 그 치마는 나에게 더 이상 맞지 않는다.

① The skirt who I bought last year doesn't fit me anymore.
② The skirt that I bought last year doesn't fit me anymore.

개념확인문제 002 다음 우리말에 맞게 순서를 바로잡아 영작하시오.

the crops / the water / Soil / need / stores	땅은 작물들이 필요로 하는 물을 저장한다.

 A 다음 문장에서 밑줄 친 부분을 알맞게 해석하시오.

> 보기
>
> I know the man <u>whom his parents are proud of</u>.
> 그의 부모님들이 자랑스러워하는

1 I collect everything <u>which my boss recommends</u>.

_____

2 The museum has some rules <u>which you should keep</u>.

_____

3 The service <u>that my friends complained about</u> was not that bad.

_____

B 괄호 안의 단어들을 순서에 맞게 써서 문장을 완성하시오.

1 He is a doctor (everyone | whom | respects).

➡ He is a doctor _____ .

2 She forgot to bring the letter (mom | that | wrote | her).

➡ She forgot to bring the letter _____ .

3 He likes the bag (brother | like | his | which | doesn't).

➡ He likes the bag _____ .

 C 다음 문장을 우리말로 해석하시오.

1 I don't remember the name of the man / with whom I talked on the phone.

➡

2 An ecosystem is a community of all the living things / which they live in.

➡

84

혼공완성

A ▶ 사진을 보고 주어진 단어들의 순서를 바로잡아 문장을 완성하시오.

1

that | This | I | is | the seafood restaurant | like

．．

2

is | that | Math | don't | most students | the subject | like

．．

B ▶ 주어진 단어들의 순서를 바로잡아 문장을 완성하시오.

1 countries | they | They | have | remember | traveled to

➡

2 I | which | visited | is | London | last year | the city

➡

3 that | The actor | wanted | I | waved | to see | to me

➡

C ▶ 알맞은 관계대명사를 활용하여 다음 ❶과 ❷, ❸과 ❹를 각각 연결하시오.

❶ Some birds can hear sounds.

❷ People cannot hear the sounds.

❸ Designers used the skills.

❹ They had learned them from building bridges.

(1) + (2) _____

(3) + (4) _____

A 우리말 의미를 참고하여 빈칸을 알맞게 채우시오.

🔍 잘 모르겠다면 ... 83페이지로

1 나는 그가 나를 위해 사주었던 꽃들을 사랑한다.

I _____ the _____ which he bought for me.

2 그 가수는 대부분의 십대들이 좋아하는 유명한 케이팝 스타이다.

The _____ is a famous K-pop star whom most teenagers _____ .

3 내가 작년에 샀던 그 치마는 나에게 더 이상 맞지 않는다.

The skirt that I _____ last year doesn't _____ me anymore.

4 땅은 작물들이 필요로 하는 물을 저장한다.

Soil _____ the water the _____ need.

B 다음 우리말에 맞게 순서를 바로잡아 영작하시오.

🔍 잘 모르겠다면 ... 84페이지로

1 나는 그의 부모님들이 자랑스러워하는 그 남자를 안다.
whom | I | his parents | the man | know | are | proud of

➡

2 그는 모든 사람들이 존경하는 의사이다.
everyone | is | he | a doctor | whom | respects

➡

3 그녀는 그녀의 엄마가 썼던 편지를 가져갈 것을 잊어버렸다.
mom | the letter | forgot | that | she | to bring | wrote | her

➡

4 생태계는 그들이 살아가는 모든 살아있는 것들의 공동체이다.
a community | an ecosystem | is | live in | of all the living things | which | they

➡

주어진 단어들의 순서를 바로잡아 문장을 완성하시오. 　🔍 잘 모르겠다면 ··· 85페이지로

1 that | this | I | is | the seafood restaurant | like

➡

2 is | that | math | don't | most students | the subject | like

➡

3 countries | they | they | have | remember | traveled to

➡

4 I | which | visited | is | London | last year | the city

➡

5 that I | the actor | wanted | waved | to see | to me

➡

D 다음 ❶~❹의 우리말 뜻을 적으시오. 　🔍 잘 모르겠다면 ··· 85페이지로

❶ Some birds can hear sounds.

❷ People cannot hear the sounds.

❸ Designers used the skills.

❹ They had learned them from building bridges.

1 _____

2 _____

3 _____

4 _____

관계대명사 – 소유격

혼공기초

**Tom has a cat /
whose eyes are blue.**
Tom은 고양이를 키운다 / 눈이 파란색인

혼공개념
001

관계대명사를 쓰면서 두 문장을 합칠 때, 생략된 단어가 소유격 대명사 자리라면 소유격 관계대명사를 써요. 선행사가 사람일 때는 관계대명사 **whose**를 쓴답니다.

I like the singer whose voice is soft.

I saw a girl whose hair came down to her waist.

He is a lawyer whose desire is to help poor people.

The boy whose mom is from India is popular
in our soccer club.

선행사가 사물이거나 동물인 경우에는 소유격 관계대명사로 보통 **whose, of which**를 쏜답니다. 아참 의문사 **whose**는 '누구의'라고 해석되니 소유격 관계대명사와 차이점이 있어요.

I found a dog whose feet were badly hurt.

He bought an old car of which the windows are already broken.

He brought a hundred roses of which the color was red.

Tell him whose cookies you'll make first. 의문사

개념확인문제 001 다음 우리말에 맞게 영작한 것을 고르시오.

1 Tom은 눈이 파란색인 고양이를 키운다.

① Tom has a cat who eyes are blue.
② Tom has a cat whose eyes are blue.

2 나는 머리카락이 그녀의 허리까지 내려오는 한 소녀를 보았다.

① I saw a girl whom hair came down to her waist.
② I saw a girl whose hair came down to her waist.

3 그는 창문이 이미 깨진 한 오래된 차를 샀다.

① He bought an old car of which the windows are already broken.
② He bought an old car off which the windows are already broken.

개념확인문제 002 다음 우리말에 맞게 순서를 바로잡아 영작하시오.

found / I / were / a dog / whose / feet / badly hurt	나는 그것의 다리가 심하게 다친 개 한 마리를 발견했다.

➡

89

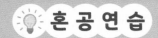 혼공연습

 다음 문장에서 밑줄 친 부분을 알맞게 해석하시오.

> 보기
> I met a woman whose dream is to build a school in Africa.
> 꿈은 아프리카에 학교를 짓는 것이다

1. There are a lot of animals whose lives are in great danger.

   _____

2. The house whose door has been replaced is over there.

   _____

3. The boy whose wallet was stolen called the police.

   _____

 괄호 안의 단어들을 순서에 맞게 써서 문장을 완성하시오.

1. She is the student (in my class | the best | whose | handwriting | is).
   ➡

2. Try to find somebody (full | whose | is | of happiness | life).
   ➡

3. There was a man (was | whose | stained | white shirt | with blood).
   ➡

 다음 문장을 우리말로 해석하시오.

1. There is a basketball player / whose height is over 210cm.

   ➡

2. The designer created a house / whose lights turn on automatically.

   ➡

A 사진을 보고 주어진 단어들의 순서를 바로잡아 문장을 완성하시오.

1

prefer | a little bitter | I | coffee | taste | whose | is

....

2

I | whose | short | that girl | know | hair | is

....

B 주어진 단어들의 순서를 바로잡아 문장을 완성하시오.

1 a lion | There's | skin | is | whose | white

➡

2 has | whose | a cat | nose | is | She | pink

➡

3 There | whose | name | was | was | a little boy | Benjamin Franklin

➡

C 알맞은 관계대명사를 활용하여 다음 ❶과 ❷, ❸과 ❹를 각각 연결하시오.

❶ The movie is about a girl.
❷ Her father works in the space station.
❸ There are many animals in Africa.
❹ Their lives are in danger.

(1) + (2) _____

(3) + (4) _____

A 우리말 의미를 참고하여 빈칸을 알맞게 채우시오.

잘 모르겠다면 ⋯→ 89페이지로

① Tom은 눈이 파란색인 고양이를 키운다.

Tom ＿＿＿＿＿＿＿＿ a cat ＿＿＿＿＿＿＿ eyes are blue.

② 나는 머리카락이 그녀의 허리까지 내려오는 한 소녀를 보았다.

I ＿＿＿＿＿＿＿＿ a girl whose hair came down to her ＿＿＿＿＿＿＿ .

③ 그는 창문이 이미 깨진 한 오래된 차를 샀다.

He bought an old car of ＿＿＿＿＿＿＿ the windows are already ＿＿＿＿＿＿＿ .

④ 나는 다리가 심하게 다친 개 한 마리를 발견했다.

I ＿＿＿＿＿＿＿＿ a dog whose ＿＿＿＿＿＿＿ were badly hurt.

B 다음 우리말에 맞게 순서를 바로잡아 영작하시오.

잘 모르겠다면 ⋯→ 90페이지로

1 목숨이 위험에 처한 동물들이 많이 있다.
are | are | a lot of | animals | there | whose | in great danger | lives

➡

2 삶이 행복으로 가득찬 누군가를 찾으려고 노력해라.
full | to find | whose | is | try | somebody | of happiness | life

➡

3 키가 210cm 이상 되는 한 농구 선수가 있다.
is | there | a basketball player | over 210cm | height | whose | is

➡

4 그 디자이너는 불이 자동으로 켜지는 한 집을 만들어냈다.
created | the designer | automatically | a house | lights | whose | turn on

➡

C 주어진 단어들의 순서를 바로잡아 문장을 완성하시오. 🔍 잘 모르겠다면 ··· 91페이지로

1 prefer | a little bitter | I | coffee | taste | whose | is

➡

2 I | whose | short | that girl | know | hair | is

➡

3 a lion | there's | skin | is | whose | white

➡

4 has | whose | a cat | nose | is | she | pink

➡

5 there | whose | name | was | was | a little boy | Benjamin Franklin

➡

D 다음 ❶~❹의 우리말 뜻을 적으시오. 🔍 잘 모르겠다면 ··· 91페이지로

❶ The movie is about a girl.
❷ Her father works in the space station.
❸ There are many animals in Africa.
❹ Their lives are in danger.

1 _____

2 _____

3 _____

4 _____

관계부사 – when, where, why, how

혼공기초

This is the hotel / where we stayed last summer.

이것은 호텔이다 / 우리가 지난 여름에 묵었던

혼공개념 001

관계대명사를 쓰면서 두 문장을 합칠 때, 선행사의 특성에 맞게 '전치사 + 관계대명사'를 한 단어로 바꾸어 쓸 수 있답니다. 이것을 관계부사라고 하고 선행사가 시간, 장소를 나타낼 때 각각 when, where을 쓰면 됩니다.

Come and see us any time when you're in town.

I can't remember the date when we took a trip to London.

Can you guess the place where I've stayed?

This park is a perfect place where children can play.

방법, 이유와 관계된 관계부사에는 각각 **how, why**가 있어요. 단, 방법을 나타내는 관계부사 **how**와 선행사 **the way**는 동시에 쓸 수 없으니 참고 하세요.

I will tell you **the way** I make lemonade with lemon juice.

I can't understand **how** he solved the problem.

What's the reason **why** you are always late?

Do you know the reason **why** Tom was absent from school?

개념확인문제 001 다음 우리말에 맞게 영작한 것을 고르시오.

1 이것은 우리가 지난 여름에 묵었던 호텔이다.

　① This is the hotel when we stayed last summer.
　② This is the hotel where we stayed last summer.

2 당신이 마을에 있을 때가 언제든 우리를 보러 와라.

　① Come and see us any time when you're in town.
　② Come and see us any time where you're in town.

3 당신이 항상 늦는 이유는 무엇인가요?

　① What's the reason why you are always late?
　② What's the reason what you are always late?

개념확인문제 002 다음 우리말에 맞게 순서를 바로잡아 영작하시오.

can't / I / how / he / solved / understand / the problem	나는 그가 어떻게 그 문제를 해결했는지 이해할 수 없다.

 혼공연습

 A 다음 문장에서 밑줄 친 부분을 알맞게 해석하시오.

> 보기
> I'll never forget the day when I met you.
> 내가 너를 만났던 그날을

(1) Can you show me the way you play badminton?

_____

(2) July is the month when it is usually the hottest.

_____

(3) He told the court how the accident happened.

_____

 B 괄호 안의 단어들을 순서에 맞게 써서 문장을 완성하시오.

(1) I remember the moment (you | to | first talked | when | me).

➡

(2) We didn't forget the day (knocked | when | he | on the door).

➡

(3) We couldn't understand (solved | how | the math problem | the kids).

➡

C 다음 문장을 우리말로 해석하시오.

(1) The nest is a place / where he attracts his mate.

➡

(2) There are also pajama parties / where kids learn the night behavior of the animals.

➡

96

A 사진을 보고 주어진 단어들의 순서를 바로잡아 문장을 완성하시오.

1

can post | made | a website | she | Her dad | where | cooking videos

....

2

is | working now | the gas station | That | where | I'm

....

B 주어진 단어들의 순서를 바로잡아 문장을 완성하시오.

1 need | how | at the table | Children | they | to know | should eat

➡

2 became | are | the reason | why | I | You | stronger

➡

3 People | often | take | why | they | time | lose | to understand

➡

C ❶~❹의 괄호 안에서 어법상 알맞은 것을 골라 아래에 쓰시오.

❶ Home is the place [when / where] you can take a rest.
❷ This is the house [when / where] I was born.
❸ There may be times [when / where] you do not achieve your goals.
❹ Knowing the reasons [why / what] you failed will help you improve your chances.

① _____ ② _____ ③ _____ ④ _____

A 우리말 의미를 참고하여 빈칸을 알맞게 채우시오.   잘 모르겠다면 ⋯ 95페이지로

(1) 이것은 우리가 지난 여름에 묵었던 호텔이다.

This is the hotel _____ we _____ last summer.

(2) 당신이 마을에 있을 때가 언제든 우리를 보러 와라.

Come and see us anytime _____ you're in _____ .

(3) 당신이 항상 늦는 이유는 무엇인가요?

What's the reason _____ you are always _____ ?

(4) 나는 그가 어떻게 그 문제를 해결했는지 이해할 수 없다.

I can't understand _____ he _____ the problem.

B 다음 우리말에 맞게 순서를 바로잡아 영작하시오.   잘 모르겠다면 ⋯ 96페이지로

(1) 나는 내가 너를 만났던 그날을 절대 잊지 않을 것이다.
I | forget | I'll | you | the day | never | when | met

➡

(2) 그는 법정에 어떻게 그 사고가 발생했는지 말했다.
the court | how | the accident | he | told | happened

➡

(3) 우리는 그가 문에 노크했던 그 날을 잊지 않았다.
didn't | when | forget | the day | knocked | we | he | on the door

➡

(4) 둥지는 그가 그의 짝을 꾀는 장소이다.
attracts | the nest | a place | where | he | is | his mate

➡

주어진 단어들의 순서를 바로잡아 문장을 완성하시오.

🔍 잘 모르겠다면 ... 97페이지로

1 can post | a website | she | her dad made | where | cooking videos

➡

2 is | working now | the gas station | that | where | I'm

➡

3 need | how | at the table | children | they | to know | should eat

➡

4 became | are | the reason | why | I | you | stronger

➡

5 people | often | take | why | they | time | lose | to understand

➡

D 다음 ❶~❹의 우리말 뜻을 적으시오.

🔍 잘 모르겠다면 ... 97페이지로

❶ Home is the place where you can take a rest.
❷ This is the house where I was born.
❸ There may be times when you do not achieve your goals.
❹ Knowing the reasons why you failed will help you improve your chances.

1 _____

2 _____

3 _____

4 _____

관계사의 계속적 용법

He likes the island, / which has wonderful beaches.

그는 그 섬을 좋아한다 / 그리고 그것은
멋진 해변을 가지고 있다

혼공개념 001

콤마 다음에 관계대명사가 와서 앞에 나온 내용에 대해 좀 더 자세한 설명을 해주는 것을 계속적 용법이라고 해요. 주로 **which, who** 등이 오고, 보통 '그리고 ~는'이라고 해석하면 자연스럽답니다. 특히 앞 문장 전체 또는 일부 내용을 뜻하는 **which**도 있으니 문맥을 잘 파악해야 해요.

Mr. Cho has two sons, who are firefighters.

Mr. Cho has two sons who are firefighters.

He designed a special helmet, which used flashing lights.

I saw a boy texting on the road, which looked really dangerous.

My uncle visited the place, where I am going to stay for a month.

He went to Hongong University, where he studied English education.

I met them on Sunday, when there was a fire in the building.

They finished the meeting at 2 p.m., when they decided to go out for lunch.

개념확인문제 001 다음 우리말에 맞게 영작한 것을 고르시오.

1 그는 그 섬을 좋아하는데, 그것은 멋진 해변을 가지고 있다.

① He likes the island, which has wonderful beaches.
② He likes the island, where has wonderful beaches.

2 Mr. Cho는 두 아들이 있는데, 그들 둘 다 소방관이다.

① Mr. Cho has two sons who are firefighters.
② Mr. Cho has two sons, who are firefighters.

3 내 삼촌은 그 장소를 방문했는데, 거기에서 나는 한 달 동안 머물 것이다.

① My uncle visited the place, which I am going to stay for a month.
② My uncle visited the place, where I am going to stay for a month.

개념확인문제 002 다음 우리말에 맞게 순서를 바로잡아 영작하시오.

was / met / in the building / them / on Sunday / , when / I / there / a fire	나는 그들을 일요일에 만났는데, 그날 그 건물에서 화재가 있었다.

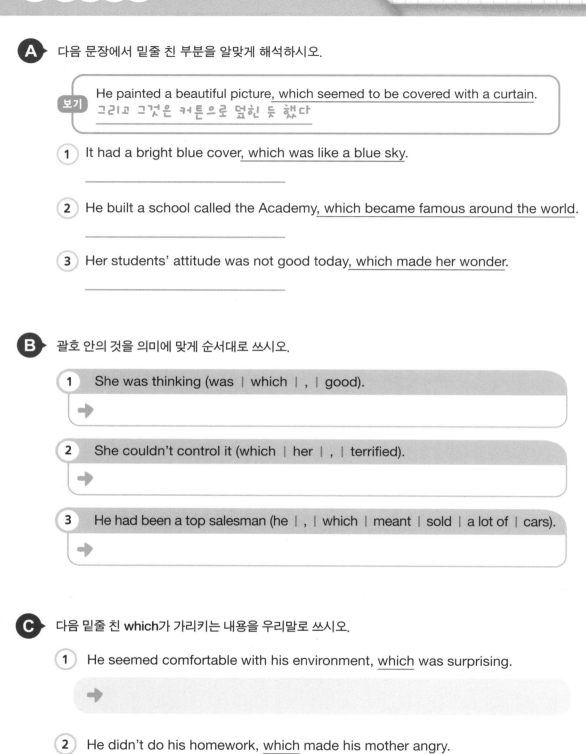

혼공연습

A 다음 문장에서 밑줄 친 부분을 알맞게 해석하시오.

> **보기** He painted a beautiful picture, which seemed to be covered with a curtain.
> 그리고 그것은 커튼으로 덮힌 듯 했다

1 It had a bright blue cover, <u>which was like a blue sky</u>.

_____

2 He built a school called the Academy, <u>which became famous around the world</u>.

_____

3 Her students' attitude was not good today, <u>which made her wonder</u>.

_____

B 괄호 안의 것을 의미에 맞게 순서대로 쓰시오.

1 She was thinking (was | which | , | good).

→

2 She couldn't control it (which | her | , | terrified).

→

3 He had been a top salesman (he | , | which | meant | sold | a lot of | cars).

→

C 다음 밑줄 친 which가 가리키는 내용을 우리말로 쓰시오.

1 He seemed comfortable with his environment, <u>which</u> was surprising.

→

2 He didn't do his homework, <u>which</u> made his mother angry.

→

사진을 보고 의미에 맞게 괄호 안의 것을 순서대로 쓰시오.

1

The human pyramid is an exercise (can | six people | be | done | with | which | ,).

···

2

Robots can work 24 hours a day (productivity | , | improves | which).

···

B 괄호 안의 것을 의미에 맞게 순서대로 쓰시오.

1 (him | , | beneath | The earth | trembled) which he took as a good sign.

➡

2 She and the others appeared healthy (surprised | which | , | Lana).

➡

3 The meat was tender (of seasoning | made up | which | , | for the lack).

➡

C 관계대명사의 계속적 용법을 활용하여 다음 ❶과 ❷, ❸과 ❹를 각각 연결하시오.

❶ Jane tried to repair her phone.
❷ But she found it impossible.
❸ He won an award at the Summer Film Festival.
❹ And it was one of the best festivals in the world.

① + ② _____

③ + ④ _____

A 우리말 의미를 참고하여 빈칸을 알맞게 채우시오.

🔍 잘 모르겠다면 ···→ 101페이지로

(1) 그는 그 섬을 좋아하는데, 그것은 멋진 해변을 가지고 있다.

He _____ the island, _____ has wonderful beaches.

(2) Mr. Cho는 두 아들이 있는데, 그들 둘 다 소방관이다.

Mr. Cho _____ two sons, _____ are firefighters.

(3) 내 삼촌은 그 장소를 방문했는데, 거기에서 나는 한 달 동안 머물 것이다.

My uncle visited the place, _____ I am going to _____ for a month.

(4) 나는 그들을 일요일에 만났는데, 그날 그 건물에서 화재가 있었다.

I met them on Sunday, _____ there was a _____ in the building.

B 다음 우리말에 맞게 순서를 바로잡아 영작하시오.

🔍 잘 모르겠다면 ···→ 102페이지로

(1) 그것은 밝은 파란색 커버를 가지고 있었는데, 그것은 파란 하늘 같았다.
it | , | which | was | had | like | a bright blue cover | a blue sky

➡

(2) 그녀는 생각하는 중이었고, 그것은 좋았다.
thinking | was | she | was | which | , | good

➡

(3) 그녀는 그것을 조절할 수 없었고, 그것은 그녀를 두렵게 했다.
couldn't | which | she | her | , | control | it | terrified

➡

(4) 그는 숙제를 하지 않았는데, 그것이 그녀의 어머니를 화나게 만들었다.
didn't do | angry | made | his mother | his homework | , | he | which

➡

C 괄호 안의 것을 의미에 맞게 순서대로 쓰시오.   🔍 잘 모르겠다면 ···→ 103페이지로

1   The human pyramid is an exercise (can | six people | be | done | with | which | ,).

➡

2   Robots can work 24 hours a day (productivity | , | improves | which).

➡

3   (him | , | beneath | the earth | trembled) which he took as a good sign.

➡

4   She and the others appeared healthy (surprised | which | , | Lana).

➡

5   The meat was tender (of seasoning | made up | which | , | for the lack).

➡

D 다음 ❶~❹의 우리말 뜻을 적으시오.   🔍 잘 모르겠다면 ···→ 103페이지로

❶ Jane tried to repair her phone.
❷ But she found it impossible.
❸ He won an award at the Summer Film Festival.
❹ And it was one of the best festivals in the world.

1 _____

2 _____

3 _____

4 _____

혼공기초

What we have / is a dream.

우리가 갖고 있는 것은 / 꿈이다

혼공개념 001

관계대명사 **what**은 **the thing which(that)**로 '~하는 것'이라는 의미예요. 주어 자리에 쓰일 경우에 '~하는 것은'으로, 목적어 자리에 쓰이면 '~하는 것을'로 해석하면 자연스러워요.

What we do not like is a lie.

What he found will amaze you.

Don't put off till tomorrow **what** you can do today.

Your dog can understand **what** you are saying.

관계대명사 **what**은 주어, 목적어 이외에도 보어, 기타 자리에 올 수 있어요. 보어는 '~하는 것이다'로 해석하면 되고, 기타는 주로 전치사 뒤에 오는 경우라는 것을 참고하세요.

We never forget what we learn with pleasure.

That is what made me upset.

I blame myself for what has happened.

There is a list of what you need.

개념확인문제 001   다음 우리말에 맞게 영작한 것을 고르시오.

1 우리가 갖고 있는 것은 꿈이다.

① What we have is a dream.
② What we have does a dream.

2 오늘 할 수 있는 일을 내일로 미루지 마라.

① Don't put off till tomorrow you can do today.
② Don't put off till tomorrow what you can do today.

3 우리는 기쁨과 함께 배우는 것을 절대 잊지 않는다.

① We never forget what we learn with pleasure.
② We never forget which we learn with pleasure.

개념확인문제 002   다음 우리말에 맞게 순서를 바로잡아 영작하시오.

myself / I / for / what / has happened / blame	나는 일어났던 일 때문에 내 자신을 비난한다.

A 다음 문장에서 밑줄 친 부분을 알맞게 해석하시오.

> 보기
>
> What is the most important to him is his daughter.
> <u>그에게 가장 중요한 것은</u>

(1) It's not about <u>what you say</u>.

_____

(2) We soon believe <u>what we desire</u>.

_____

(3) <u>What cannot be cured</u> must be endured.

_____

B 괄호 안의 것을 의미에 맞게 순서대로 쓰시오.

(1) (found | I | in the park | What) was a cute dog.

➡

(2) The axe forgets (the tree | what | remembers).

➡

(3) The tongue speaks (the heart | thinks | what).

➡

C 다음 문장을 우리말로 해석하시오.

(1) You never know / what you can do / until you try.

➡

(2) I think about what you can do / in the future.

➡

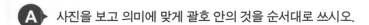

혼공완성

A 사진을 보고 의미에 맞게 괄호 안의 것을 순서대로 쓰시오.

1

(children | do | should | What | is) to go to bed early.
....

2

they | Babies | try | see | to copy | what
....

B 괄호 안의 것을 의미에 맞게 순서대로 쓰시오.

1 (you | is | had | in | What | mind) not quite clear to us.
➡

2 (don't know | got | have | We | what | we) until we lose it.
➡

3 The man was (she | about | uncertain | said | what).
➡

C 관계대명사 what을 활용하여 다음 ❶과 ❷, ❸과 ❹를 각각 연결하시오.

❶ We keep doing the thing.
❷ We have always done it.
❸ Winners do the thing.
❹ Losers don't want to do the thing.

(1) + (2) _____

(3) + (4) _____

A 우리말 의미를 참고하여 빈칸을 알맞게 채우시오.   🔍 잘 모르겠다면 ..., 107페이지로

(1) 우리가 갖고 있는 것은 꿈이다.

    _____ we _____ is a dream.

(2) 오늘 할 수 있는 일을 내일로 미루지 마라.

    Don't _____ off till tomorrow _____ you can do today.

(3) 우리는 기쁨과 함께 배우는 것을 절대 잊지 않는다.

    We never _____ what we _____ with pleasure.

(4) 나는 일어났던 일 때문에 내 자신을 비난한다.

    I _____ myself for _____ has happened.

B 다음 우리말에 맞게 순서를 바로잡아 영작하시오.   🔍 잘 모르겠다면 ..., 108페이지로

(1) 그에게 가장 중요한 것은 그의 딸이다.
is | what | to him | is | his daughter | the most important
➡

(2) 치유될 수 없는 것은 반드시 견뎌내야 한다.
cannot | must | be endured | be cured | what
➡

(3) 도끼는 나무가 기억하는 것을 잊는다.
forgets | the tree | what | the axe | remembers
➡

(4) 나는 네가 미래에 할 수 있는 것에 대해 생각한다.
what | I | you | can do | think about | in the future
➡

C 주어진 단어들을 의미에 맞게 순서대로 쓰시오. 🔍 잘 모르겠다면 ···→ 109페이지로

1 (children | do | should | what | is) to go to bed early.

➡

2 they | babies | try | see | to copy | what

➡

3 (you | is | had | in | what | mind) not quite clear to us.

➡

4 (don't know | got | have | we | what | we) until we lose it.

➡

5 The man was (she | about | uncertain | said | what).

➡

D 다음 ❶~❹의 우리말 뜻을 적으시오. 🔍 잘 모르겠다면 ···→ 109페이지로

❶ We keep doing the thing.
❷ We have always done it.
❸ Winners do the thing.
❹ Losers don't want to do the thing.

1 _____

2 _____

3 _____

4 _____

혼공기초

I will follow you /
wherever you go.
나는 당신을 따라 갈 것이다 /
당신이 어디에 가던지

혼공개념
001

관계사에 **ever**를 붙여 그 의미를 강조하는 것을 복합관계사라고 해요.
whoever, whatever, whomever 등 복합관계대명사로 쓰이는 경우,
명사가 쓰이는 곳에 올 수 있으며 각각 '~하는 사람은 누구든지', '~하는 것
은 무엇이든지', '~은 누구든지'로 해석하면 자연스러워요.

Whoever does best will get the prize.

They eat **whatever** they can find.

You can welcome **who(m)ever** you like to meet here.

Give it to **whomever** you are satisfied with.

복합관계부사를 사용한 문장은 복합관계대명사와 달리 생략하더라도 나머지 문장이 하나의 완전한 의미를 지녀요. 하나의 문장 앞, 뒤에 다 올 수 있고 '~ 하던지'라고 해석하면 자연스러워요. 'However + 형용사/부사 + 주어 + 동사'는 '아무리 ~가 ~하더라도'라는 뜻으로 자주 쓰이니 참고하세요.

Wherever I go, there you are.

I will find him wherever he may be.

I'll discuss it with you whenever you like.

However hard you try, you'll always miss out on something in life.

개념확인문제 001   다음 우리말에 맞게 영작한 것을 고르시오.

1 나는 당신이 어디에 가던지, 당신을 따라 갈 것이다.

① I will follow you whenever you go.
② I will follow you wherever you go.

2 당신은 여기서 만나고 싶은 누구든지 환영할 수 있다.

① You can welcome whoever you like to meet here.
② You can welcome whatever you like to meet here.

3 내가 어디로 가던지, 당신이 거기에 있다.

① Whenever I go, there you are.
② Wherever I go, there you are.

개념확인문제 002   다음 우리말에 맞게 순서를 바로잡아 영작하시오.

| whomever / you / Give / are / to / satisfied with / it | 그것을 당신이 만족하는 누구에게든 주어라. |

A 다음 문장에서 밑줄 친 부분을 알맞게 해석하시오.

> 보기
>
> I can do <u>whatever I want</u>.
> 내가 원하는 것은 무엇이든지

(1) <u>Whoever made this cake</u> is a real artist.

_____

(2) Some people enjoy themselves <u>wherever they are</u>.

_____

(3) <u>Whomever you select</u> will have my support.

_____

B 괄호 안의 것을 의미에 맞게 순서대로 쓰시오.

(1) (you | try to | However | persuade | hard | her), she won't leave for Seoul.

➡

(2) (I | Whenever | at | look | the picture), it gives me a warm feeling.

➡

(3) He can answer the question (it | however | hard | is).

➡

C 다음 문장을 우리말로 해석하시오.

(1) Whomever he selects, / there will be a lot of opportunities.

➡

(2) However hard she tries, / nothing seems to work.

➡

114

A 사진을 보고 의미에 맞게 괄호 안의 것을 순서대로 쓰시오.

1 Always lock your car (leave | whenever | it | you).

．．

2 (time | I | have | Whenever | free), I play the piano.

．．

B 주어진 단어들을 의미에 맞게 순서대로 쓰시오.

1 You can (like | invite | you | whomever).

➡

2 (However | be | the night | long | may), the dawn will break.

➡

3 you | can go | wherever | We | like

➡

C ❶~❹의 괄호 안에서 어법상 알맞은 것을 골라 아래에 쓰시오.

❶ I'll be there [whatever / however] happens.
❷ I don't want to see them, [whoever / however] they are.
❸ The hero was loved [whatever / wherever] he went.
❹ He won't get the result [whatever / however] hard he tries.

(1) _____ (2) _____ (3) _____ (4) _____

A 우리말 의미를 참고하여 빈칸을 알맞게 채우시오.   🔍 잘 모르겠다면 ···→ 113페이지로

① 나는 당신이 어디에 가던지, 당신을 따라 갈 것이다.

I will ＿＿＿＿＿＿ you ＿＿＿＿＿＿ you go.

② 당신은 여기서 만나고 싶은 누구든지 환영할 수 있다.

You can ＿＿＿＿＿＿ whoever you like to ＿＿＿＿＿＿ here.

③ 내가 어디로 가던지, 당신이 거기에 있다.

＿＿＿＿＿＿ I go, there ＿＿＿＿＿＿ are.

④ 그것을 당신이 만족하는 누구에게든 주어라.

＿＿＿＿＿＿ it to whomever you are ＿＿＿＿＿＿ with.

B 다음 우리말에 맞게 순서를 바로잡아 영작하시오.   🔍 잘 모르겠다면 ···→ 114페이지로

1 나는 내가 원하는 것은 무엇이든지 할 수 있다.
I | I | can | want | do | whatever

➡

2 어떤 사람들은 그들이 어디에 있던지 즐겁게 보낸다.
enjoy | they | some | themselves | people | wherever | are

➡

3 그것이 아무리 어렵더라도 그는 그 질문에 대답할 수 있다.
it | however | he | the question | can answer | hard | is

➡

4 아무리 열심히 그녀가 노력하더라도, 아무것도 제대로 되지 않는 듯 하다.
tries | , | nothing | she | seems | hard | however | to work

➡

C 주어진 단어들을 의미에 맞게 순서대로 쓰시오.

1. Always lock your car (leave | whenever | it | you).

   ➡

2. (time | I | have | whenever | free), I play the piano.

   ➡

3. You can (like | invite | you | whomever).

   ➡

4. (however | be | the night | long | may), the dawn will break.

   ➡

5. you | can go | wherever | we | like

   ➡

D 다음 ❶~❹의 우리말 뜻을 적으시오.

❶ I'll be there whatever happens.
❷ I don't want to see them, whoever they are.
❸ The hero was loved wherever he went.
❹ He won't get the result however hard he tries.

1. _____

2. _____

3. _____

4. _____

대상의 확장
비교 표현

Everest 8,848 m (29,029 ft)
K2 8,611 m (28,251 ft)
Kangchenjunga 8,586 m (28,169 ft)
Lhotse 8,516 m (27,940 ft)
Makalu 8,485 m (27,838 ft)
Cho Oyu 8,188 m (26,864 m)
Dhaulagiri I 8,167 m (26,795 ft)
Manaslu 8,163 m (26,781 ft)
Nanga Parbat 8,126 m (26,660 ft)
Annapurna I 8,091 m (26,545 ft)
Gasherbrum I 8,080 m (26,509 ft)
Broad Peak 8,051 m (26,414 ft)
Gasherbrum II 8,034 m (26,358 ft)
Shishapangma 8,027 m (26,335 ft)

비교급

The moon is drier / than a desert.

달은 더 건조하다 / 사막보다

혼공개념 001

다른 대상과 비교하면서 대상을 설명하는 것을 비교급이라고 해요. '더 ~ 한'이라고 해석하고, 형용사 + (e)r의 형태 또는 특정 형용사나 3음절 이상 의 긴 형용사는 앞에 **more**를 씁니다. 주로 '비교급 than ~'으로 쓰여서 '~보다 더 ~ 한'이라는 의미로 해석해요.

Actions speak louder than words.

The two of you will be closer than the others.

He is paid less than he really earns.

Children who give thanks feel more positive than those who don't.

경우에 따라서는 단어 앞에 **more**를 붙이거나, 형용사 + **(e)r**의 형태가 아닌 불규칙 비교급도 있어요. 아울러, **much, far, a lot, still**은 비교급 앞에서 '훨씬'이라는 의미로 강조를 나타낸답니다. '**the** 비교급 ~, **the** 비교급'은 '~하면 할수록 더욱 ~ 하다'라는 비교급 표현으로 꼭 알아두세요.

A liar is worse than a thief.

The honest penny is better than the stolen dollar.

Flying squirrels are much smaller than tree squirrels.

The more we do, the more we can do.

개념확인문제 001 다음 우리말에 맞게 영작한 것을 고르시오.

1 달은 사막보다 더 건조하다.

① The moon is drier than a desert.
② The moon is more drier than a desert.

2 너희들 둘은 다른 사람들보다 더 가까워질 거야.

① The two of you will be closer the others.
② The two of you will be closer than the others.

3 날다람쥐들은 나무다람쥐들보다 훨씬 더 작다.

① Flying squirrels are very smaller than tree squirrels.
② Flying squirrels are much smaller than tree squirrels.

개념확인문제 002 다음 우리말에 맞게 순서를 바로잡아 영작하시오.

is / than / a thief / worse / A liar	거짓말쟁이는 도둑보다 더 나쁘다.

A 다음 문장에서 밑줄 친 부분을 알맞게 해석하시오.

> 보기
> They are <u>healthier and happier</u> than those who don't exercise.
> <u>그들은 더 건강하고 더 행복하다</u>

(1) She's <u>younger</u> than him.

_____

(2) <u>The first one would be easier</u> than other choices.

_____

(3) I think <u>robots are better than human workers</u>.

_____

B 괄호 안의 것을 의미에 맞게 순서대로 쓰시오.

(1) It (was | he | much | than | higher | could reach).
➡ It   .

(2) She (faster | than | is | that boy).
➡ She   .

(3) Two heads (than | better | one | are).
➡ Two heads   .

C 다음 문장을 우리말로 해석하시오.

(1) The truth is more complicated / than we think.
➡

(2) The more we study, / the more we discover our ignorance.
➡

혼공완성

A 사진을 보고 의미에 맞게 괄호 안의 것을 순서대로 쓰시오.

1.
A TV show (funnier | than | is | a documentary).
....

2.
A barking dog (than | is | a sleeping lion | better).
....

B 주어진 단어들의 순서를 바로잡아 문장을 완성하시오.

1. Alex | more | comfortable | seemed | at home | than at work
   ➡

2. important | more | Safety | is | than texting
   ➡

3. faster | than | He | runs | far | his brother
   ➡

C 밑줄 친 부분을 주어진 의미와 알맞은 비교급으로 고치시오.

❶ Teenagers are often expected to go to bed <u>early</u> than adults do. (더 일찍)

❷ The fresher the apple is, the <u>good</u> it tastes. (더 좋은)

❸ Grateful children are <u>likely</u> to help others. (더 ~하는 경향이 있는)

❹ Do you want to be <u>close</u> to your father? (더 가까운)

1 _____ 2 _____ 3 _____ 4 _____

A 우리말 의미를 참고하여 빈칸을 알맞게 채우시오.

잘 모르겠다면 ···› 121페이지로

(1) 달은 사막보다 더 건조하다.

The   is   than a desert.

(2) 너희들 둘은 다른 사람들보다 더 가까워질 거야.

The two of you will be   than the   .

(3) 날다람쥐들은 나무다람쥐들보다 훨씬 더 작다.

Flying squirrels are much   the tree squirrels.

(4) 거짓말쟁이는 도둑보다 더 나쁘다.

A   is   than a thief.

B 다음 우리말에 맞게 순서를 바로잡아 영작하시오.

잘 모르겠다면 ···› 122페이지로

(1) 그들은 운동하지 않는 사람들보다 더 건강하고 행복하다.
healthier | don't exercise | and | are | happier | than | those | they | who

➡

(2) 나는 로봇들이 인간 직원들보다 더 낫다고 생각한다.
robots | are | think | better | I | than human workers

➡

(3) 그것은 그가 닿을 수 있는 것보다 훨씬 더 높았다.
was | he | much | it | than | higher | could reach

➡

(4) 진실은 우리가 생각하는 것보다 더 복잡하다.
is | think | complicated | the truth | than | we | more

➡

C 주어진 단어들을 의미에 맞게 순서대로 쓰시오. 잘 모르겠다면 ···→ 123페이지로

1 A TV show (funnier | than | is | a documentary).

➡

2 A barking dog (than | is | a sleeping lion | better).

➡

3 Alex | more | comfortable | seemed | at home | than at work

➡

4 important | more | safety | is | than texting

➡

5 faster | than | he | runs | far | his brother

➡

D 다음 ❶~❹의 우리말 뜻을 적으시오. 잘 모르겠다면 ···→ 123페이지로

❶ Teenagers are often expected to go to bed earlier than adults do.
❷ The fresher the apple is, the better it tastes.
❸ Grateful children are more likely to help others.
❹ Do you want to be closer to your father?

1 _____

2 _____

3 _____

4 _____

원급비교

혼공기초

We can run / as fast as him.
우리는 달릴 수 있다 / 그만큼 빨리

혼공개념
001

비교 대상과 능력이 거의 같을 때 원급비교를 사용해요. 'as 형용사(부사) as'로 나타내며 '~만큼 ~한'이라고 해석해요. 아울러 배수 표현인 ~ times, twice 등을 앞에 써서 차이가 나는 정도를 나타낼 수 있답니다.

Today is as stormy as yesterday.

Her class has as many students as mine.

She is not as diligent as her mother.

He makes two times as much money as his friends.

비교 대상에 명사, 대명사 외에도 문장 등이 올 수 있어요. 아울러 '가능한 한 ~ 한(하게)'라는 관용표현 'as ~ as possible', 'as ~ as 주어 + can'도 있으니 알아두세요.

She will give you as much work as you want.

Run as fast as you can go.

It was as weird as it was shocking.

I'll call you as soon as possible.

개념확인문제 001 다음 우리말에 맞게 영작한 것을 고르시오.

1 우리는 그만큼 빨리 달릴 수 있다.

① We can run as fast as him.
② We can run as faster as him.

2 그녀는 그녀의 어머니만큼 부지런하지는 않다.

① She is as not diligent as her mother.
② She is not as diligent as her mother.

3 네가 갈 수 있는 만큼 빨리 달려라.

① Run as fast as you can go.
② Run faster than you can go.

개념확인문제 002 다음 우리말에 맞게 순서를 바로잡아 영작하시오.

| two times / as / makes / much money / his friends / as / He | 그는 그의 친구들이 버는 돈의 두 배만큼 번다. |

A 다음 문장에서 밑줄 친 부분을 알맞게 해석하시오.

> 보기
> I'm as hungry as a horse.
> 말만큼 배고픈
> _____

(1) It will all happen as quickly as a wink.

_____

(2) It's not as simple as it looks.

_____

(3) Blow up the balloon until it gets as big as an egg.

_____

B 괄호 안의 것을 의미에 맞게 순서대로 쓰시오.

(1) A man is (as | he | as | old | feels).

➡ A man is _____ .

(2) Their fur (as | white | as | is | snow).

➡ Their fur _____ .

(3) Making cakes (as | as | is | making | easy | cookies).

➡ Making cakes _____ .

C 다음 문장을 우리말로 해석하시오.

(1) Ecosystems can be as big as the whole world / and as tiny as a rock.

➡

(2) She still looks as sad / as she did 3 weeks ago.

➡

A 사진을 보고 의미에 맞게 괄호 안의 것을 순서대로 쓰시오.

1

There were (in the department store | as | 1000 people | many | as).

....

2

She loves (the zoo | do | as | as | I | much).

....

B 주어진 단어들의 순서를 바로잡아 문장을 완성하시오.

1 not | easy | as | This may | be | as | it | sounds
➡

2 as | she | hungry | as | was exhausted | She | was
➡

3 four times | as | is | The African continent | as | large | the European one
➡

C 다음은 현서의 TV에 대한 보고서 중 일부이다. 우리말 의미와 일치하도록 원급비교를 활용하여 빈칸에 들어갈 내용을 알맞게 영작하시오.

Television

Early television was in black and white,

and the quality _____ it is today.

초기 텔레비전은 흑백이었다.
그리고 그 품질은 오늘날만큼 좋지 않았다.

A 우리말 의미를 참고하여 빈칸을 알맞게 채우시오.

잘 모르겠다면 …→ 127페이지로

(1) 우리는 그만큼 빨리 달릴 수 있다.

We can _____ as _____ as him.

(2) 그녀는 그녀의 어머니만큼 부지런하지는 않다.

She is _____ as _____ as her mother.

(3) 네가 갈 수 있는 만큼 빨리 달려라.

_____ as fast _____ you can go.

(4) 그는 그의 친구들이 버는 돈의 두배만큼 번다.

He _____ two _____ as much money as his friends.

B 다음 우리말에 맞게 순서를 바로잡아 영작하시오.

잘 모르겠다면 …→ 128페이지로

1 그것은 보이는 것만큼 단순하지 않다.
not | as | it's | as | it | simple | looks

➡

2 그것들의 털은 눈만큼 하얗다.
as | white | as | is | their fur | snow

➡

3 케익 만드는 것은 쿠키 만드는 것만큼 쉽다.
cakes | as | as | is | making | making | easy | cookies

➡

4 그녀는 3주 전에 그랬던 것만큼 여전히 슬퍼 보인다.
as | sad | looks | as | she | she | did | 3 weeks | still | ago

➡

C 주어진 단어들의 순서를 바로잡아 문장을 완성하시오.

잘 모르겠다면 …→ 129페이지로

1 in the department store | as | there | were | 1000 people | many | as

➡

2 the zoo | she | loves | do | as | as | I | much

➡

3 not | easy | as | this may | be | as | it | sounds

➡

4 as | she | hungry | as | was exhausted | she | was

➡

5 four times | as | is | the African continent | as | large | the European one

➡

D 다음 ❶~❹의 우리말 뜻을 적으시오.

잘 모르겠다면 …→ 129페이지로

❶ Early television was in black and white.
❷ The quality was not as good as it is today.
❸ She will give you as much work as you want.
❹ I'll call you as soon as possible.

(1) _____

(2) _____

(3) _____

(4) _____

최상급/관용적 표현

혼공기초

**It was the tallest building /
in the world until 1930.**

그것은 가장 높은 건물이었다 /
1930년까지 전 세계에서

**혼공개념
001**

셋 이상의 대상에서 '가장 ~한'이라는 의미를 갖는 것을 최상급이라고 해요.
'형용사 + est'의 형태가 많고, 단어 앞에 **most, least**를 붙이기도 해요.
'**one of the** 최상급 + 복수명사'는 '가장 ~한 것 중 하나'라는 뜻으로 최상의
표현을 나타낸답니다.

Mt. Everest is the highest mountain in the world.

I have just seen the most perfect show.

He has the least money of us all.

**Einstein is one of the best scientists
in history.**

'부정어구 + 원급비교(**as~as**)'를 써서 '어떤 ~도 ~만큼 ~하지 않다'라는 최상의 의미를 표현할 수 있어요. 물론 '비교급 + **than any other** 단수명사'를 써도 '다른 어떤 것보다 더 ~하다'라는 최상의 의미를 표현할 수 있어요.

No other US city is as big as New York.

Nothing is as sad as her new song.

Steve is taller than any other student in the class.

Love is more precious than any other thing.

개념확인문제 001 다음 우리말에 맞게 영작한 것을 고르시오.

1 그것은 1930년까지 전 세계에서 가장 높은 건물이었다.

① It was the tallest building in the world until 1930.
② It was the most tall building in the world until 1930.

2 나는 방금 가장 완벽한 쇼를 보았다.

① I have just seen the perfectest show.
② I have just seen the most perfect show.

3 어떤 것도 그녀의 새 노래만큼 슬프지 않다.

① Nothing is as sad as her new song.
② Nothing is not as sad as her new song.

개념확인문제 002 다음 우리말에 맞게 순서를 바로잡아 영작하시오.

history / the best scientists / is / one / Einstein / of / in

Einstein은 역사상 최고의 과학자들 중 한 명이다.

 다음 문장에서 밑줄 친 부분을 알맞게 해석하시오.

> 보기 February is the shortest month of the year.
> 연중 가장 짧은 달이다

(1) The population of China is the largest in the world.

_____

(2) Honesty is one of the most important things in our lives.

_____

(3) No other person is more positive than my mom.

_____

B 괄호 안의 단어들을 순서에 맞게 써서 문장을 완성하시오.

(1) He (my class | the second | is | boy | in | tallest).
➡ _____

(2) Running (one | is | of | to lose | ways | the most | effective | weight).
➡ _____

(3) This (serves | food | in this area | the most | restaurant | delicious).
➡ _____

C 다음 문장을 우리말로 해석하시오.

(1) No other person is as energetic / as James is.

➡

(2) A tortoise is one of the slowest animals / in the world.

➡

혼공완성

A 사진을 보고 주어진 단어들의 순서를 바로잡아 문장을 완성하시오.

1

the longest | is | river | the United States | in | The Mississippi

....

2

are | in the world | the most | expensive | Diamonds | gemstones

....

B 주어진 단어들의 순서를 바로잡아 문장을 완성하시오.

1 than | any | A whale | other | is | mammal | larger

2 selfless | as | is | as | No | other | Captain America | superhero

3 is | than | The Amazon | other | river | any | larger | in the world

C 다음은 현서가 수업 시간에 발표할 조사내용이다. 각 문장이 최상을 의미하도록 밑줄 친 부분을 알맞게 고쳐서 쓰시오.

❶ The cobra is one of the world's deadliest <u>snake</u>.

❷ Helsinki is one of the <u>colder</u> cities in the world.

❸ Elephants are one of the smartest <u>an animal</u> in the world.

❹ Martin Luther King Jr. was one of the <u>importanter</u> people in American history.

① _____ ② _____ ③ _____ ④ _____

135

혼공복습

A 우리말 의미를 참고하여 빈칸을 알맞게 채우시오. 🔍 잘 모르겠다면 … 133페이지로

(1) 그것은 1930년까지 전 세계에서 가장 높은 건물이었다.

It was the _____ building in the world _____ 1930.

(2) 나는 방금 가장 완벽한 쇼를 보았다.

I have just _____ the _____ perfect show.

(3) 어떤 것도 그녀의 새 노래만큼 슬프지 않다.

_____ is as _____ as her new song.

(4) Einstein은 역사상 최고의 과학자들 중 한명이다.

Einstein is _____ of the best _____ in history.

B 다음 우리말에 맞게 순서를 바로잡아 영작하시오. 🔍 잘 모르겠다면 … 134페이지로

(1) 2월은 연중 가장 짧은 달이다.
of the year | is | month | the shortest | February

➡

(2) 정직은 우리 삶에서 가장 중요한 것들 중 하나이다.
is | honesty | one | the most | of | things | important | in our lives

➡

(3) 그는 우리 반에서 두번째로 가장 키가 큰 소년이다.
my class | the second | is | boy | he | in | tallest

➡

(4) 다른 어떤 사람도 James만큼 에너지가 넘치지 않는다.
as | person | is | is | energetic | no | as | other | James

➡

C 주어진 단어들의 순서를 바로잡아 문장을 완성하시오.　　🔍 잘 모르겠다면 ⋯ 135페이지로

1　the longest ｜ is ｜ river ｜ the United States ｜ in ｜ the Mississippi

➡

2　are ｜ in the world ｜ the most ｜ expensive ｜ diamonds ｜ gemstones

➡

3　than ｜ any ｜ a whale ｜ other ｜ is ｜ mammal ｜ larger

➡

4　selfless ｜ as ｜ is ｜ as ｜ no ｜ other ｜ Captain America ｜ superhero

➡

5　is ｜ than ｜ the Amazon ｜ other ｜ river ｜ any ｜ larger ｜ in the world

➡

D 다음 ❶~❹의 우리말 뜻을 적으시오.　　🔍 잘 모르겠다면 ⋯ 135페이지로

❶ The cobra is one of the world's deadliest snakes.

❷ Helsinki is one of the coldest cities in the world.

❸ Elephants are one of the smartest animals in the world.

❹ Martin Luther King Jr. was one of the most important people in American history.

(1)

(2)

(3)

(4)

Part 5

★ Special ★
60문장

1

농구하는 것은 아주 신난다.

12쪽

2

안전벨트를 착용하는 것은 법으로 요구된다.

15쪽

3

내가 공원에서 발견했던 것은 한 귀여운 개였다.

15쪽

4

그녀는 축구 선수가 되는 것을 바랐다.

18쪽

5

그녀는 그녀의 지역사회에서 요리 수업을 가르치는 것을 시작했다.

21쪽

6

그 과학자들은 무엇이 잘못되었는지를 알아냈다.

21쪽

7

건강을 유지하는 것은 중요하다.

24쪽

8

Sean이 우리 동아리에 가입할 수 없다는 것은 슬프다.

27쪽

9

미국 사람들이 거실에서 신발을 신는 것은 괜찮다.

27쪽

10

그는 공룡에 관심을 가지게 되었다.

30쪽

11

에펠 탑은 파리에서 가장 유명한 구조물 중 하나이다.

33쪽

12

Sue는 그가 늦을 거라 예상했다.

33쪽

13  나는 그 산에 오르는 것을 시작했다.

38쪽

14 아침을 먹는 것은 아이들을 위해서 아주 중요하다.

41쪽

15 그의 직업은 다른 사탕들의 맛을 서술하는 것이다.

41쪽

16 곤돌라 타기는 Venice를 보는 놀라운 방법이다.

44쪽

17 그 이론을 테스트하기 위한 몇 가지 이유들이 있다.

47쪽

18   좋은 공원은 개들을 건강하게 유지시킬 훌륭한 방법이 될 것이다.

47쪽

19

몇몇 화산 과학자들은 사람들에게 경고하기 위해서 거기에 있었다.

50쪽

20

마카롱은 매일 먹기에는 너무나 달다.

53쪽

21

춤은 중요한 행사를 기념하기 위해 종종 사용된다.

53쪽

22

이 커플은 1월에 결혼할 것이다.

56쪽

23

다음 기차는 3시 정각에 출발할 예정이다.

59쪽

24

그 시험은 허리케인 때문에 연기될 것이다.

59쪽

25

내 어머니께서 한 흥미로운 이야기를 나에게 말해주셨다.

62쪽

26

이것은 쓰나미라고 불리는 빠른 파도를 만들어낸다.

65쪽

27

의사들은 균형잡힌 식단의 핵심은 다양성이라고 말한다.

65쪽

28

분홍색으로 옷을 입어서, 그녀는 장미처럼 보였다.

68쪽

29

파티에 초대받았기 때문에, 소녀들은 새 옷을 위해 쇼핑을 갔다.

71쪽

30

쉬운 한국어로 쓰여졌기 때문에, 그 책은 베스트셀러가 되었다.

71쪽

31  당신에게 너무 큰 자전거를 타지 마세요.   🔍 76쪽

32 나는 파란색 스웨터를 입었던 그 소년을 기억한다.   🔍 79쪽

33 한 남자는 아주 성공한 가게를 하나 가지고 있었다.   🔍 79쪽

34 나는 그가 나를 위해 사주었던 꽃들을 사랑한다.   🔍 82쪽

35  이곳은 내가 좋아하는 해산물 식당이다.   🔍 85쪽

36  수학은 대부분의 학생들이 좋아하지 않는 과목이다.   🔍 85쪽

145

37

Tom은 눈이 파란색인 고양이를 키운다.

88쪽

38

나는 맛이 약간 쓴 커피를 선호한다.

91쪽

39

나는 머리가 짧은 저 소녀를 안다.

91쪽

40

이것은 우리가 지난 여름에 묵었던 호텔이다.

94쪽

41

그녀의 아빠는 그녀가 요리 동영상을 올릴 수 있는 웹사이트를 만들었다.

97쪽

42

저것은 내가 지금 일하고 있는 주유소이다.

97쪽

43

그는 그 섬을 좋아하는데, 그것은 멋진 해변을 가지고 있다.

100쪽

44

인간 피라미드는 하나의 운동인데, 그것은 여섯 명으로 행해질 수 있다.

103쪽

45

로봇들은 하루에 24시간을 일할 수 있는데, 그것은 생산성을 향상시켜 준다.

103쪽

46

우리가 갖고 있는 것은 꿈이다.

106쪽

47

아이들이 해야 하는 것은 일찍 자러 가는 것이다.

109쪽

48

아이들은 보는 것을 그대로 따라 하려고 애쓴다.

109쪽

49

나는 당신이 어디에 가던지 당신을 따라 갈 것이다.

112쪽

50

당신이 그것을 언제 두던지 당신의 차를 항상 잠궈라.

115쪽

51

내가 여가 시간이 있을 때는 언제나, 나는 피아노를 연주한다.

115쪽

52

달은 사막보다 더 건조하다.

120쪽

53

TV 쇼는 다큐멘터리보다 더 재미있다.

123쪽

54

짖는 개가 잠자는 사자보다 더 낫다.

123쪽

55 우리는 그만큼 빨리 달릴 수 있다.

126쪽

56 그 백화점에는 1000명 정도 많은 사람들이 있었다.

129쪽

57 그녀는 내가 사랑하는 만큼 그 동물원을 사랑한다.

129쪽

58 그것은 1930년까지 전 세계에서 가장 높은 건물이었다.

132쪽

59 미시시피 강은 미국에서 가장 길다.

135쪽

60 다이아몬드는 세계에서 가장 비싼 보석이다.

135쪽

Answers
정답

Answer · 정답

개념확인문제 001 본문 13쪽

1 ② 2 ② 3 ②

개념확인문제 002 본문 13쪽

Where he came from is unknown.

혼공연습 본문 14쪽

A ① 한 달에 책 열 권을 읽는 것은
② 야채를 먹는 것은
③ 그 팀이 지난밤에 경기에서 이겼다는 것은

B ① true love is difficult
② I passed the exam is unbelievable
③ breakfast is very important for children/
breakfast for children is very important

C ① 항상 "그래"라고 대답하는 것은 / 너의 우정을 빠뜨
릴 수 있다 / 위험에
② 그가 이사간다는 것은 / 다음 주에 / 사실이다

혼공완성 본문 15쪽

A ① To wear a seat belt is required by law.
② What I found in the park was a cute dog.

B ① Following someone's SNS was annoying
to me.
② Advertising the product can increase sales.
③ To smoke is one of the major causes of
cancer.

C 잘못된 것 　　　바른 표현
① 　　→　　 was
④ 　　→　　 means

혼공복습 본문 16쪽

A ① Playing, exciting
② Walking, tiring
③ leaving, shock
④ Where, unknown

B ① Eating vegetables is good for your health.
② Finding true love is difficult.
③ That I passed the exam is unbelievable.
④ Having breakfast is very important for
children.

C ① To wear a seat belt is required by law.
② What I found in the park was a cute dog.
③ Following someone's SNS was annoying
to me.
④ Advertising the product can increase sales.
⑤ To smoke is one of the major causes of cancer.

D ① 이 실험을 위한 팀에 과학자 한 명은 Tim이었다.
② 내 여동생에 의해 만들어진 프렌치 프라이는 짜지 않다.
③ 현명하지 않은 것은 위험하다.
④ 행복해지는 것은 나에게 많은 의미가 있다.

개념확인문제 001 본문 19쪽

1 ② 2 ① 3 ②

개념확인문제 002 본문 19쪽

No one knows what will happen in the future.

혼공연습 본문 20쪽

A ① 추수 감사절을 위한 칠면조 한 마리를
② 해외에서 공부하는 것의 어려움을
③ 그녀가 프랑스어를 말할 수 있는지를

B ① painted her self-portrait with a paintbrush
② bought the picture at a great cost
③ raised her hand above her head

C ① 그는 궁금해한다 / 부자들이 정말 행복한지를
② 너는 원하게 될 것이다 / 새로운 목표들을 세우는 것과
/ 새로운 것들에 도전하는 것을

혼공완성 본문 21쪽

A ① She started teaching cooking classes in her
community.
② The scientists figured out what went wrong.

B ① Phillip doesn't know what happened to Janet.
② I'll tell you why I chose this subject.
③ She doesn't care how she dresses.

C 잘못된 것 　　　바른 표현
① 　　→　　 playing
④ 　　→　　 if(whether)

A ① desired, be
② stopped, strength
③ know, disappearing
④ knows, happen

B ① They discussed the difficulty of studying abroad.
② I bought the picture at a great cost.
③ He wonders if the rich are really happy.
④ You will want to set new goals and to try new things.

C ① She started teaching cooking classes in her community.
② The scientists figured out what went wrong.
③ Phillip doesn't know what happened to Janet.
④ I'll tell you why I chose this subject.
⑤ She doesn't care how she dresses.

D ① 헨리는 바이올린을 연주하는 것을 즐긴다.
② 그녀는 열심히 공부하기로 결심했다.
③ 많은 사람들은 네 잎이 있는 클로버가 행운이라고 믿는다.
④ 나는 그가 집에 있는지 없는지 모른다.

DAY 03 가주어/가목적어

1 ② 2 ② 3 ①

He made it clear that we should leave.

A ① 물에서 떠있는 것은
② "아니오"라고 말하고 왜인지 설명하는 것이
③ 자정 전에 십대들이 잠에 드는 것은

B ① thought it hard to become a teacher
② is natural for parents to want to protect their children
③ is true that some habits are bad for us

C ① 그의 태도는 / 어렵게 만들었다 / 함께 일하는 것을
② 많은 사람들은 / 중요하다고 여기지 않는다 / 재활용하는 것을

A ① It is sad that Sean cannot join our club.
② It is fine for Americans to wear shoes in a living room.

B ① It is very important to exercise regularly.
② This machine makes it possible to increase efficiency.
③ The weather made it difficult for them to stay warm.

C 번호: ②
해석: 앤디는 컴퓨터를 고치는 것이 거의 불가능하다는 것을 발견했다.

A ① It, stay
② surprising, mammals
③ rain, difficult
④ it, leave

B ① It is possible to float in water.
② I thought it hard to become a teacher.
③ His attitude made it difficult to work together.
④ Many people don't consider it important to recycle.

C ① It is sad that Sean cannot join our club.
② It is fine for Americans to wear shoes in a living room.
③ It is very important to exercise regularly.
④ This machine makes it possible to increase efficiency.
⑤ The weather made it difficult for them to stay warm.

D ① 흥미로운 어떤 것을 선택하는 것은 좋은 생각이다.
② 앤디는 컴퓨터를 고치는 것이 거의 불가능하다는 것을 발견했다.
③ 어떤 도움도 없이 너의 숙제를 하는 것은 어렵다.
④ 소년이 호루라기 소리를 듣는 것은 어려웠다.

DAY 04 다양한 보어

개념확인문제 001 　　　　　 본문 31쪽

1 ②　2 ①　3 ②

개념확인문제 002 　　　　　 본문 31쪽

Mr. Park allowed Jerry to go home early.

혼공연습 　　　　　 본문 32쪽

A ① 천천히 움직이는 것이었다
② 항상 나쁜 것은 아니다
③ 전화상에서 이상하게 들렸다

B ① keeps our bones healthy
② saw him singing in the rain
③ felt something crawling on my body

C ① 그의 목표는 / 새로운 어떤 것을 배우는 것이다
② 그것은 만들 것이다 / 이웃을 더 밝은 곳으로

혼공완성 　　　　　 본문 33쪽

A ① The Eiffel Tower is one of the most famous structures in Paris.
② Sue expected him to be late.

B ① The problem is that we have no money.
② It sometimes made him a little unhappy.
③ They had the file stolen in the elevator.
They had stolen the file in the elevator.

C ① O.C.　② O.C.　③ C　④ O.C.

혼공복습 　　　　　 본문 34쪽

A ① interested, dinosaurs
② soup, tastes
③ named, child
④ allowed, go

B ① This mission turned out impossible.
② Her voice sounded strange on the phone.
③ We saw him singing in the rain.
④ It will make the neighborhood a brighter place.

C ① The Eiffel Tower is one of the most famous structures in Paris.
② Sue expected him to be late.
③ The problem is that we have no money.
④ It sometimes made him a little unhappy.

⑤ They had the file stolen in the elevator.
They had stolen the file in the elevator.

D ① 우리는 옳고 그름을 가리는 것이 어렵다는 것을 알게 된다.
② 내 여동생은 내가 그녀의 컴퓨터를 사용하는 것을 허락해 주었다.
③ 그는 에베레스트 산 정상에 도달한 첫 번째 맹인이 되었다.
④ 이것은 그들이 나중에 그들의 삶에서 성공하도록 돕는다.

DAY 05 to 부정사의 명사적 용법/동명사

개념확인문제 001 　　　　　 본문 39쪽

1 ②　2 ②　3 ①

개념확인문제 002 　　　　　 본문 39쪽

Do you enjoy watching horror movies?

혼공연습 　　　　　 본문 40쪽

A ① 모든 개들을 돕는 것이다
② 더 따뜻하고 더 안전한 장소들로 이동하는 것을
③ 공부하는 것을 마치지 않았다

B ① favorite thing is to lie on the grass
② expected to go shopping early in the morning
③ don't want to wear a uniform

C ① 너는 아마 원하지 않을 것이다 / 너의 아버지와 낚시하러 가는 것을
② 긍정적으로 생각하는 것은 / 도와줄 수도 있다 / 네가 스트레스를 다루는 것을

혼공완성 　　　　　 본문 41쪽

A ① Having breakfast is very important for children.
② His job is to describe the flavor of different candies.

B ① Eating vegetables is good for your health.
② Practicing interview questions is helpful.
③ To wear a seat belt is required by law.

C ① using　② to go　③ to do　④ to have

A
① began, climb
② learn, myself
③ mind, recipe
④ enjoy, watching

B
① She avoided answering the questions.
② My favorite thing is to lie on the grass.
③ You may not want to go fishing with your father.
④ Thinking positively could help you deal with stress.

C
① Having breakfast is very important for children.
② His job is to describe the flavor of different candies.
③ Eating vegetables is good for your health.
④ Practicing interview questions is helpful.
⑤ To wear a seat belt is required by law.

D
① 그는 그것을 사용하는 것을 멈추기로 결심했다.
② 나는 오늘 밤에 크리스와 영화를 보러 가기로 약속했다.
③ 이번 주말에 어떤 것을 하기로 계획했니?
④ 요즘에는 많은 사람들이 애완 동물을 기르는 것을 선택한다.

DAY 06 to 부정사의 형용사적 용법

개념확인문제 001 본문 45쪽

1 ② 2 ① 3 ②

개념확인문제 002 본문 45쪽

The police officer was looking for something to write with.

혼공연습 본문 46쪽

A
① 서로 소통할 대단한 방법이다
② 방문할 많은 역사적인 장소들을
③ 운전할 차를 가지고 있지 않다

B
① has given us ideas to improve our happiness
② had some problems to solve
③ have something to tell you

C
① 부끄러움을 극복하는 최선의 방법은 / 자신감을 갖는 것이다
② 그들은 잠재력을 가지고 있다 / 좋은 친구가 될

혼공완성 본문 47쪽

A
① There are a few reasons to test the theory.
② A good park would be a great way to keep dogs healthy.

B
① Tomorrow is the time to say goodbye to everyone.
② Anna needs some money to spend.
③ These are great ways to save the environment.

C ① on ② on ③ about ④ with

혼공복습 본문 48쪽

A
① amazing, to
② needed, drink
③ house, live
④ looking, with

B
① They don't have a car to drive.
② She has given us ideas to improve our happiness.
③ The best way to overcome shyness is to have confidence.
④ They have the potential to become good friends.

C
① There are a few reasons to test the theory.
② A good park would be a great way to keep dogs healthy.
③ Tomorrow is the time to say goodbye to everyone.
④ Anna needs some money to spend.
⑤ These are great ways to save the environment.

D
① 어머니는 나에게 쓸 한 장의 종이를 주셨다.
② 우리는 앉을 의자가 없다.
③ 이것이 말할 주제이다.
④ 마이크는 같이 놀 친구가 많다.

DAY 07 to 부정사의 부사적 용법

개념확인문제 001 본문 51쪽

1 ② 2 ② 3 ①

⑤ People use dance to express themselves.

개념확인문제 002 〔본문 51쪽〕

The chair is too big to carry on my own.

혼공연습 〔본문 52쪽〕

A ① 그의 생일을 너에게 상기시켜주기 위해서
② 상황을 좀 더 낫게 만들기 위해서
③ 설상가상으로

B ① closed the window not to disturb my wife
② need about 40 different nutrients to stay healthy
③ made paintings of birds to raise money

C ① 이 새로운 모델은 충분히 작다 / 주머니에 딱 들어갈 만큼
② 그녀의 부모님은 충격받았다 / 그녀가 학교를 그만두었다는 것을 알고

혼공완성 〔본문 53쪽〕

A ① Macarons are too sweet to eat every day.
② Dance is often used to celebrate an important event.

B ① Dishonesty is impossible to hide.
② Most parents wake up quickly to take care of their babies.
③ People use dance to express themselves.

C ① 목적 ② 감정의 원인 ③ 문장 전체 수식 ④ 결과

혼공복습 〔본문 54쪽〕

A ① volcano, warn
② happy, see
③ grew, be
④ too, carry

B ① She ran after the bus to get back her umbrella.
② I closed the window not to disturb my wife.
③ This new model is small enough to fit in a pocket.
④ Her parents were shocked to find out she quit school.

C ① Macarons are too sweet to eat every day.
② Dance is often used to celebrate an important event.
③ Dishonesty is impossible to hide.
④ Most parents wake up quickly to take care of their babies.

D ① 이 필수적인 영양소들을 얻기 위해서는, 너는 너의 음식 선택에 반드시 균형을 맞춰야 한다.
② 제임스는 그를 다시 봐서 기뻤다.
③ 분명히, K-pop은 전 세계에서 인기를 얻고 있다.
④ 내 할아버지는 80살까지 사셨다.

DAY 08 to 부정사의 be to 용법

개념확인문제 001 〔본문 57쪽〕

1 ② **2** ① **3** ②

개념확인문제 002 〔본문 57쪽〕

No one was to be seen in the town.

혼공연습 〔본문 58쪽〕

A ① 성공할 것이다 / 성공할 수 있다
② 국제 회의에 참석할 것이다
③ 만약 우리가 성공하려면

B ① are to wear a mask in this operating room
② is to visit New York for the cooking festival
③ is to go back to her home by midnight

C ① 아무것도 / 발견할 수 없었다
② 모든 사람은 / 언젠가 죽을 것이다

혼공완성 〔본문 59쪽〕

A ① The next train is to depart at three o'clock.
② The exam is to be delayed because of the hurricane.

B ① People are to wash their hands.
② He is to become a great scientist.
③ The Olympic Games are to be held next year.

C ① to leave ② to wait ③ to give ④ to touch

혼공복습 〔본문 60쪽〕

A ① couple, married
② clean, room
③ was, be
④ one, seen

B ① The president is to attend an international conference next month.

② You are to wear a mask in this operating room.
③ She is to go back to her home by midnight
④ Nothing was to be found.

C ① The next train is to depart at three o'clock.
② The exam is to be delayed because of the hurricane.
③ People are to wash their hands.
④ He is to become a great scientist.
⑤ The Olympic Games are to be held next year.

D ① 그 회장은 회의를 위해 파리를 떠날 것이다.
② 그들은 저 다리를 이용하기 위해 내년까지 기다려야 한다.
③ 정원사들은 그것을 꽃피우기 위해 그것에 물을 더 주어야 한다.
④ 너는 실험실에서 어떠한 도구도 만져서는 안 된다.

DAY 09 분사

개념확인문제 001 『본문 63쪽』
1 ② 2 ② 3 ①

개념확인문제 002 『본문 63쪽』
Earth's largest recorded earthquake struck Chile.

혼공연습 『본문 64쪽』

A ① 항상 붐빈다
② 나라들의 이름을 딴 섬들을 사기 위해
③ 생각하기에 너무 두렵다

B ① heard her name called
② enjoyed the amazing views of the city at night
③ heard about the damage caused by the oil spill

C ① 범인은 피하려고 노력했다 / 당황스러운 질문을
② 원숭이가 한 마리 있었다 / 바위에 앉아 있는

혼공완성 『본문 65쪽』

A ① This creates a fast wave called a tsunami.
② Doctors say that the key to a balanced diet is variety.

B ① My 13-year-old son tried to jump over a parked car.
② She saw her neighbor standing there.
③ The coins have ruined one of nature's wonders.
The coins have one of nature's wonders ruined.

C ① dressed ② expected ③ singing
④ exciting

혼공복습 『본문 66쪽』

A ① told, interesting
② quit, boring
③ confused, math
④ recorded, struck

B ① The movie theater next to the school is always crowded.
② She heard her name called.
③ The criminal tried to avoid an embarrassing question.
④ There was a monkey sitting on a rock.

C ① This creates a fast wave called a tsunami.
② Doctors say that the key to a balanced diet is variety.
③ My 13-year-old son tried to jump over a parked car.
④ She saw her neighbor standing there.
⑤ The coins have ruined one of nature's wonders.
The coins have one of nature's wonders ruined.

D ① 공연 시작 한 시간 전에 나는 옷을 입었다.
② 이것은 실제로 예상된 결과였습니다.
③ 그들은 근처의 연못들에서 개구리들이 노래부르는 것을 들을 수 있다.
④ 이 영화는 신나고 재미있어 보인다.

DAY 10 분사구문

개념확인문제 001 『본문 69쪽』
1 ① 2 ② 3 ②

개념확인문제 002 본문 69쪽

Left alone at the zoo, the boy started to cry.

혼공연습 본문 70쪽

Ⓐ ① 프랑스에 살기 때문에
② 피곤해서
③ 서랍을 열었을 때

Ⓑ ① Not knowing his number
② Excited to hear the news
③ Having seen the movie on TV recently

Ⓒ ① 돈이 거의 없었기 때문에 / 그녀는 새 차를 살 여유가
없었다
② 늦고 싶지 않았기 때문에 / 나는 학교에 택시를 타고
갔다

혼공완성 본문 71쪽

Ⓐ ① Invited to a party
② Written in easy Korean

Ⓑ ① Surprised by a loud scream
② repeating my lines
③ Exhausted from so much exercise

Ⓒ ① doing ② Having ③ Born ④ Brought

혼공복습 본문 72쪽

Ⓐ ① Dressed, like
② Not, silent
③ Having, nothing
④ Left, cry

Ⓑ ① Living in France, she speaks French fluently.
② Feeling tired, I went to bed early.
③ Not knowing his number, I couldn't call him.
④ Not wanting to be late, I took a taxi to
school.

Ⓒ ① Excited to hear the news
② Having seen the movie on TV recently
③ Written in easy Korean
④ Surprised by a loud scream
⑤ Exhausted from so much exercise

Ⓓ ① 이 활동을 하는 동안에 대화가 자연스럽게 일어날 것
이다.
② 작은 몸을 가지고 있기 때문에 붉은 늑대는 무게가
약 20킬로그램 정도 나간다.
③ 태국에서 2001년도에 태어난 Hong은 그림 그리는
법을 2005년에 배우기 시작했다.

④ 여행에서 가져와진 그 예쁜 유리잔은 저기에 전시되
어 있었다.

DAY
11 관계대명사 – 주격

개념확인문제 001 본문 77쪽

1 ② 2 ① 3 ②

개념확인문제 002 본문 77쪽

The cat which is sitting on the fence looks very
scary.

혼공연습 본문 78쪽

Ⓐ ① 수학을 잘하는 한 소녀를
② 매우 흥미로운 책들을
③ 탁자 위에 있는 과일들을

Ⓑ ① who had always wanted to be an astronaut
② who is sleeping on the bed
③ who teaches students at school

Ⓒ ① 친밀한 관계를 맺고 있는 십대들은 / 그들의 가족과 /
운이 좋다
② 학교 근처에 사는 사람들은 / 빨리 운전을 하지 않는
법을 금방 배운다

혼공완성 본문 79쪽

Ⓐ ① I remember the boy who wore a blue sweater.
② A man had a shop that was very successful.

Ⓑ ① He met a boy who had hearing difficulties.
② Mr. Gordon was a teacher who worked at
a little village school.
③ Having someone who listens to you at
school can really help.

Ⓒ ① + ② Each coin has blocked the small holes
that give the pool its heat.
③ + ④ There once was a king who was
defeated in a battle.

혼공복습 본문 80쪽

Ⓐ ① ride, that
② know, wearing
③ Find, hair
④ that(which), looks

B ① My sister who lives in Canada is a biologist.
② Tito is a businessman who had always wanted to be an astronaut.
③ Look at the cute baby who is sleeping on the bed.
④ A teacher is a person who teaches students at school.

C ① I remember the boy who wore a blue sweater.
② A man had a shop that was very successful.
③ He met a boy who had hearing difficulties.
④ Mr. Gordon was a teacher who worked at a little village school.
⑤ Having someone who listens to you at school can really help.

D ① 동전 하나하나가 작은 구멍들을 막았다.
② 그것들은 웅덩이에 열을 준다.
③ 한 때 왕이 있었다.
④ 그는 전쟁에서 패배했다.

DAY 12 관계대명사 – 목적격

개념확인문제 001 본문 83쪽

1 ② 2 ① 3 ②

개념확인문제 002 본문 83쪽

Soil stores the water the crops need.

혼공연습 본문 84쪽

A ① 나의 상사가 추천하는
② 당신이 지켜야 하는
③ 나의 친구가 불평했던

B ① whom everyone respects
② that her mom wrote
③ which his brother doesn't like

C ① 나는 그 남자의 이름을 기억하지 못한다 / 내가 전화로 이야기 나눴던
② 생태계는 모든 살아있는 것들의 공동체이다 / 그들이 살아가는

혼공완성 본문 85쪽

A ① This is the seafood restaurant that I like.
② Math is the subject that most students don't like.

B ① They remember countries they have traveled to.
② London is the city which I visited last year.
③ The actor that I wanted to see waved to me.

C ① + ② Some birds can hear sounds (that) people cannot hear.
③ + ④ Designers used the skills (that) they had learned from building bridges.

혼공복습 본문 86쪽

A ① love, flowers
② singer, like
③ bought, fit
④ stores, crops

B ① I know the man whom his parents are proud of.
② He is a doctor whom everyone respects.
③ She forgot to bring the letter that her mom wrote.
④ An ecosystem is a community of all living things which they live in.

C ① This is the seafood restaurant that I like.
② Math is the subject that most students don't like.
③ They remember countries they have traveled to.
④ London is the city which I visited last year.
⑤ The actor that I wanted to see waved to me.

D ① 어떤 새들은 소리를 들을 수 있다.
② 사람들은 그 소리를 들을 수 없다.
③ 디자이너들은 기술을 사용했다.
④ 그들은 다리를 건설하면서 그것들을 배웠었다.

DAY 13 관계대명사 – 소유격

개념확인문제 001 본문 89쪽

1 ② 2 ② 3 ①

개념확인문제 002 본문 89쪽

I found a dog whose feet were badly hurt.

혼공연습 〈본문 90쪽〉

Ⓐ ① 목숨이 큰 위험에 처해있다
② 문이 교체되었다
③ 지갑을 도둑맞았다

Ⓑ ① whose handwriting is the best in my class
② whose life is full of happiness
③ whose white shirt was stained with blood

Ⓒ ① 한 농구 선수가 있다/ 키가 210cm 이상 되는
② 그 디자이너는 한 집을 만들어냈다 / 불이 자동으로
켜지는

혼공완성 〈본문 91쪽〉

Ⓐ ① I prefer coffee whose taste is a little bitter.
② I know that girl whose hair is short.

Ⓑ ① There's a lion whose skin is white.
② She has a cat whose nose is pink.
③ There was a little boy whose name was
Benjamin Franklin.

Ⓒ ① + ② The movie is about a girl whose father
works in the space station.
③ + ④ There are many animals in Africa
whose lives are in danger.

혼공복습 〈본문 92쪽〉

Ⓐ ① has, whose
② saw, waist
③ which, broken
④ found, feet

Ⓑ ① There are a lot of animals whose lives are
in great danger.
② Try to find somebody whose life is full of
happiness.
③ There is a basketball player whose height
is over 210cm.
④ The designer created a house whose lights
turn on automatically.

Ⓒ ① I prefer coffee whose taste is a little bitter.
② I know that girl whose hair is short.
③ There's a lion whose skin is white.
④ She has a cat whose nose is pink.
⑤ There was a little boy whose name was
Benjamin Franklin.

Ⓓ ① 그 영화는 한 소녀에 대한 것이다.
② 그녀의 아버지는 우주 정거장에서 일한다.
③ 아프리카에는 많은 동물들이 있다.
④ 그들의 목숨이 위험에 처해있다.

DAY 14 관계부사 – when, where, why, how

개념확인문제 001 〈본문 95쪽〉

1 ② 2 ① 3 ①

개념확인문제 002 〈본문 95쪽〉

I can't understand how he solved the problem.

혼공연습 〈본문 96쪽〉

Ⓐ ① 네가 배드민턴을 치는 방법을
② 보통 가장 더운 달이다
③ 어떻게 사고가 일어났는지

Ⓑ ① when you first talked to me
② when he knocked on the door
③ how the kids solved the math problem

Ⓒ ① 둥지는 장소이다 / 그가 그의 짝을 꾀는
② 파자마 파티도 또한 있다 / 아이들이 동물들의 야행
행동을 배우는

혼공완성 〈본문 97쪽〉

Ⓐ ① Her dad made a website where she can
post cooking videos.
② That is the gas station where I'm working
now.

Ⓑ ① Children need to know how they should
eat at the table.
② You are the reason why I became stronger.
③ People often take time to understand why
they lose.

Ⓒ ① where ② where ③ when ④ why

혼공복습 〈본문 98쪽〉

Ⓐ ① where, stayed
② when, town
③ why, late
④ how, solved

B ① I'll never forget the day when I met you.
② He told the court how the accident happened.
③ We didn't forget the day when he knocked on the door.
④ The nest is a place where he attracts his mate.

C ① Her dad made a website where she can post cooking videos.
② That is the gas station where I'm working now.
③ Children need to know how they should eat at the table.
④ You are the reason why I became stronger.
⑤ People often take time to understand why they lose.

D ① 집은 당신이 휴식을 취할 수 있는 장소이다.
② 이곳은 내가 태어났던 집이다.
③ 당신이 목표를 달성하지 못하는 순간들이 있을 수 있습니다.
④ 당신이 실패했던 이유들을 아는 것은 당신의 가능성을 향상시키는데 도움을 줄 것입니다.

DAY 15 관계사의 계속적 용법

개념확인문제 001 (본문 101쪽)

1 ① 2 ② 3 ②

개념확인문제 002 (본문 101쪽)

I met them on Sunday, when there was a fire in the building.

혼공연습 (본문 102쪽)

A ① 그리고 그것은 파란 하늘같았다
② 그리고 그것은 전 세계적으로 유명해졌다
③ 그리고 그것은 그녀를 궁금하게 만들었다

B ① , which was good
② , which terrified her
③ , which meant he sold a lot of cars

C ① 그가 그의 환경에 편안한 것처럼 보였던 것
② 그가 그의 숙제를 하지 않았던 것

혼공완성 (본문 103쪽)

A ① , which can be done with six people
② , which improves productivity

B ① The earth trembled beneath him,
② , which surprised Lana
③ , which made up for the lack of seasoning

C ① + ② Jane tried to repair her phone, which she found impossible.
③ + ④ He won an award at the Summer Film Festival, which was one of the best festivals in the world.

혼공복습 (본문 104쪽)

A ① likes, which
② has, who
③ where, stay
④ when, fire

B ① It had a bright blue cover, which was like a blue sky.
② She was thinking, which was good.
③ She couldn't control it, which terrified her.
④ He didn't do his homework, which made his mother angry.

C ① , which can be done with six people
② , which improves productivity
③ The earth trembled beneath him,
④ , which surprised Lana
⑤ , which made up for the lack of seasoning

D ① 제인은 그녀의 휴대폰을 고치려고 노력했다.
② 그러나 그녀는 그것이 불가능하다는 것을 알았다.
③ 그는 여름 영화제에서 상을 받았다.
④ 그리고 그것은 전 세계의 최고 축제들 중 하나였다.

DAY 16 관계대명사 – what

개념확인문제 001 (본문 107쪽)

1 ① 2 ② 3 ①

개념확인문제 002 (본문 107쪽)

I blame myself for what has happened.

혼공연습 （본문 108쪽）

Ⓐ ① 당신이 말하는 것
② 우리가 바라는 것을
③ 치유될 수 없는 것은

Ⓑ ① What I found in the park
② what the tree remembers
③ what the heart thinks

Ⓒ ① 당신은 결코 알 수 없다 / 당신이 할 수 있는 것을 /
당신이 시도할 때까지는
② 나는 네가 할 수 있는 것에 대해 생각한다 / 미래에

혼공완성 （본문 109쪽）

Ⓐ ① What children should do is
② Babies try to copy what they see.

Ⓑ ① What you had in mind is
② We don't know what we have got
③ uncertain about what she said

Ⓒ ① + ② We keep doing what we have always
done.
③ + ④ Winners do what losers don't want to
do.

혼공복습 （본문 110쪽）

Ⓐ ① What, have
② put, what
③ forget, learn
④ blame, what

Ⓑ ① What is the most important to him is his
daughter.
② What cannot be cured must be endured.
③ The axe forgets what the tree remembers.
④ I think about what you can do in the future.

Ⓒ ① What children should do is
② Babies try to copy what they see
③ What you had in mind is
④ We don't know what we have got
⑤ uncertain about what she said

Ⓓ ① 우리는 계속 그것을 하고 있다.
② 우리는 항상 그것을 해왔다.
③ 승자들은 그것을 한다.
④ 패자들은 그것을 하는 것을 원하지 않는다.

DAY 17 복합관계사

개념확인문제 001 （본문 113쪽）

1 ② 2 ① 3 ②

개념확인문제 002 （본문 113쪽）

Give it to whomever you are satisfied with.

혼공연습 （본문 114쪽）

Ⓐ ① 이 케익을 만든 사람은 누구든지
② 그들이 어디에 있던지
③ 당신이 선택하는 사람이 누구든지

Ⓑ ① However hard you try to persuade her
② Whenever I look at the picture
③ however hard it is

Ⓒ ① 그가 선택하는 사람이 누구든지 / 많은 기회들이 있
을 것이다
② 그녀가 아무리 열심히 노력하더라도 / 아무것도 효과
가 없는 것처럼 보인다

혼공완성 （본문 115쪽）

Ⓐ ① whenever you leave it
② Whenever I have free time

Ⓑ ① invite whomever you like
② However long the night may be
③ We can go wherever you like.

Ⓒ ① whatever ② whoever ③ wherever
④ however

혼공복습 （본문 116쪽）

Ⓐ ① follow, wherever
② welcome, meet
③ Wherever, you
④ Give, satisfied

Ⓑ ① I can do whatever I want.
② Some people enjoy themselves wherever
they are.
③ He can answer the question however hard
it is.
④ However hard she tries, nothing seems to
work.

C ① whenever you leave it
② Whenever I have free time
③ invite whomever you like
④ However long the night may be
⑤ We can go wherever you like.
　 You can go wherever we like.

D ① 무슨 일이 일어나던지 나는 거기에 있을 것이다.
② 그들이 누구든지 나는 그들이 보고 싶지 않다.
③ 그 영웅은 어디를 가던지 사랑받았다.
④ 그가 아무리 열심히 노력하더라도, 그는 그 결과를 얻지 못할 것이다.

DAY 18 비교급

개념확인문제 001 　(본문 121쪽)

1 ① **2** ② **3** ②

개념확인문제 002 　(본문 121쪽)

A liar is worse than a thief.

혼공연습 　(본문 122쪽)

A ① 그녀는 더 어리다
② 첫 번째 것이 더 쉬울 것이다
③ 로봇이 인간 직원들보다 더 나을 것이다

B ① was much higher than he could reach
② is faster than that boy
③ are better than one

C ① 진실은 더 복잡하다 / 우리가 생각하는 것보다
② 우리가 더 많이 공부할수록 / 우리의 무지를 더 많이 발견한다

혼공완성 　(본문 123쪽)

A ① is funnier than a documentary
② is better than a sleeping lion

B ① Alex seemed more comfortable at home than at work.
② Safety is more important than texting.
③ He runs far faster than his brother.

C ① earlier　② better　③ more likely　④ closer

혼공복습 　(본문 124쪽)

A ① moon, drier
② closer, others
③ smaller, than
④ liar, worse

B ① They are healthier and happier than those who don't exercise.
② I think robots are better than human workers.
③ It was much higher than he could reach.
④ The truth is more complicated than we think.

C ① is funnier than a documentary
② is better than a sleeping lion
③ Alex seemed more comfortable at home than at work.
④ Safety is more important than texting.
⑤ He runs far faster than his brother.

D ① 십대들은 종종 어른들보다 더 일찍 잠자리에 들 것으로 예상된다.
② 사과가 더 신선할수록, 더 맛이 좋다.
③ 감사하는 아이들은 더 남을 돕는 경향이 있다.
④ 당신은 당신의 아버지와 더 가까워지기를 원합니까?

DAY 19 원급비교

개념확인문제 001 　(본문 127쪽)

1 ① **2** ② **3** ①

개념확인문제 002 　(본문 127쪽)

He makes two times as much money as his friends.

혼공연습 　(본문 128쪽)

A ① 눈 깜짝할 만큼 빨리
② 보이는 것만큼 단순하지 않은
③ 달걀만큼 커다란

B ① as old as he feels
② is as white as snow
③ is as easy as making cookies

C ① 생태계는 전 세계만큼 클 수 있고 / 바위만큼 작을 수 있다
② 그녀는 여전히 슬퍼 보인다 / 3주 전에 그녀가 그랬던 것 만큼

혼공완성 (본문 129쪽)

A ① as many as 1000 people in the department store
② the zoo as much as I do

B ① This may not be as easy as it sounds.
② She was as hungry as she was exhausted.
③ The African continent is four times as large as the European one.

C was not as good as

혼공복습 (본문 130쪽)

A ① run, fast
② not, diligent
③ Run, as
④ makes, times

B ① It's not as simple as it looks.
② Their fur is as white as snow.
③ Making cakes is as easy as making cookies.
④ She still looks as sad as she did 3 weeks ago.

C ① There were as many as 1000 people in the department store.
② She loves the zoo as much as I do.
③ This may not be as easy as it sounds.
④ She was as hungry as she was exhausted.
⑤ The African continent is four times as large as the European one.

D ① 초기 텔레비전은 흑백이었다.
② 품질이 오늘날만큼 좋지 않았다.
③ 그녀는 당신에게 당신이 원하는 만큼 많은 일을 줄 것이다.
④ 나는 가능한 빨리 너에게 전화할 것이다.

DAY 20 최상급 / 관용적 표현

개념확인문제 001 (본문 133쪽)

1 ① 2 ② 3 ①

개념확인문제 002 (본문 133쪽)

Einstein is one of the best scientists in history.

혼공연습 (본문 134쪽)

A ① 세계에서 가장 많다
② 가장 중요한 것들 중 하나이다
③ 다른 어떤 사람도 더 긍정적이지는 않다

B ① is the second tallest boy in my class
② is one of the most effective ways to lose weight
③ restaurant serves the most delicious food in this area

C ① 다른 어떤 사람도 에너지가 넘치지 않는다 / James 만큼
② 거북이는 가장 느린 동물들 중 하나이다 / 세계에서

혼공완성 (본문 135쪽)

A ① The Mississippi is the longest river in the United States.
② Diamonds are the most expensive gemstones in the world.

B ① A whale is larger than any other mammal.
② No other superhero is as selfless as Captain America.
③ The Amazon is larger than any other river in the world.

C ① snakes ② coldest ③ animals
④ most important

혼공복습 (본문 136쪽)

A ① tallest, until
② seen, most
③ Nothing, sad
④ one, scientists

B ① February is the shortest month of the year.
② Honesty is one of the most important things in our lives.
③ He is the second tallest boy in my class.
④ No other person is as energetic as James is.

C ① The Mississippi is the longest river in the United States.
② Diamonds are the most expensive gemstones in the world.
③ A whale is larger than any other mammal.
④ No other superhero is as selfless as Captain America.
⑤ The Amazon is larger than any other river in the world.

D ① 코브라는 세상에서 가장 치명적인 뱀들 중 하나이다.
② 헬싱키는 세계에서 가장 추운 도시들 중 하나이다.
③ 코끼리는 세계에서 가장 똑똑한 동물들 중 하나이다.
④ 마틴 루터 킹 주니어는 미국 역사상 가장 중요한 인물들 중 한명이다.

★ Special 60 문장 ★

본문 140쪽

1 Playing basketball is very exciting.
2 To wear a seat belt is required by law.
3 What I found in the park was a cute dog.
4 She desired to become a soccer player.
5 She started teaching cooking classes in her community.
6 The scientists figured out what went wrong.
7 It is important to stay healthy.
8 It is sad that Sean cannot join our club.
9 It is fine for Americans to wear shoes in a living room.
10 He became interested in dinosaurs.
11 The Eiffel Tower is one of the most famous structures in Paris.
12 Sue expected him to be late.
13 I began to climb the mountain.
14 Having breakfast is very important for children.
15 His job is to describe the flavor of different candies.
16 A gondola ride is an amazing way to see Venice.
17 There are a few reasons to test the theory.
18 A good park would be a great way to keep dogs healthy.
19 A few volcano scientists were there to warn the people.
20 Macarons are too sweet to eat every day.
21 Dance is often used to celebrate an important event.
22 This couple is to get married in January.
23 The next train is to depart at three o'clock.
24 The exam is to be delayed because of the hurricane.
25 My mother told me an interesting story.
26 This creates a fast wave called a tsunami.
27 Doctors say that the key to a balanced diet is variety.
28 Dressed in pink, she looked like a rose.
29 Invited to a party, the girls went shopping for new clothes.
30 Written in easy Korean, the book became a best seller.
31 Do not ride a bike that is too big for you.
32 I remember the boy who wore a blue sweater.
33 A man had a shop that was very successful.
34 I love the flowers which he bought for me.
35 This is the seafood restaurant that I like.
36 Math is the subject that most students don't like.
37 Tom has a cat whose eyes are blue.
38 I prefer coffee whose taste is a little bitter.
39 I know that girl whose hair is short.
40 This is the hotel where we stayed last summer.
41 Her dad made a website where she can post cooking videos.
42 That is the gas station where I'm working now.
43 He likes the island, which has wonderful beaches.
44 The human pyramid is an exercise, which can be done with six people.
45 Robots can work 24 hours a day, which improves productivity.
46 What we have is a dream.
47 What children should do is to go to bed early.
48 Babies try to copy what they see.
49 I will follow you wherever you go.
50 Always lock your car whenever you leave it.
51 Whenever I have free time, I play the piano.
52 The moon is drier than a desert.
53 A TV show is funnier than a documentary.
54 A barking dog is better than a sleeping lion.
55 We can run as fast as him.
56 There were as many as 1000 people in the department store.
57 She loves the zoo as much as I do.
58 It was the tallest building in the world until 1930.
59 The Mississippi is the longest river in the United States.
60 Diamonds are the most expensive gemstones in the world.